CONTRIBUTORS AND CONSULTANTS

HALL BARTLETT, *Ed.D., Citizenship Education Project, Teachers College, Columbia University; Author*

WALT DISNEY, *Motion Picture and Television Producer*

EVELYN MILLIS DUVALL, *Ph.D., Author and Consultant on Family Life; Authority on Child Development*

EDNA E. EISEN, *Ph.D., Professor of Geography, Kent State University*

J. ALLEN HYNEK, *Ph.D., Associate Director, Smithsonian Astrophysical Observatory*

LELAND B. JACOBS, *Ph.D., Professor of Education, Teachers College, Columbia University*

ELEANOR M. JOHNSON, *M.A., Director of Elementary School Services, Graduate Division, Wesleyan University*

HERBERT A. LANDRY, *M.S., Ph.D., Director, Bureau of Educational Program Research and Statistics, New York City Public Schools*

MILTON LEVINE, *M.D., Associate Professor of Pediatrics, New York Hospital*

WILLY LEY, *Professor of Science, Fairleigh Dickinson University; Rocket Expert and Author*

NORMAN LLOYD, *M.A., Teacher of Literature and Materials of Music, Juilliard School of Music*

LENOX R. LOHR, *M.E., D.Eng., D.Sc., President, Museum of Science and Industry, Chicago*

WILL C. McKERN, *D.S., Former Director, Milwaukee Public Museum; Anthropologist*

RICHARD A. MARTIN, *B.S., Curator, N. W. Harris Public School Extension, Chicago Natural History Museum*

MAURICE PATE, *Executive Director, United Nations Children's Fund (UNICEF)*

NORMAN VINCENT PEALE, *D.D., LL.D., Litt.D., LH.D.; Minister, Marble Collegiate Church, New York; Author*

RUTHERFORD PLATT, *B.A., Member of Two North Pole Expeditions with Admiral MacMillan; Author of Nature Books*

ILLA PODENDORF, *M.S., Teacher of Science, University of Chicago Laboratory Schools; Author of Science Books*

MARY M. REED, *Ph.D., Supervisor of Little Golden Books; Formerly of Teachers College, Columbia University*

JOHN R. SAUNDERS, *M.A., Chairman, Department of Public Instruction, American Museum of Natural History*

GLENN T. SEABORG, *Ph.D., LL.D., D.Sc., Chancellor and Professor of Chemistry, University of California, Berkeley; Associate Director, University of California Radiation Laboratory; Co-winner of Nobel Prize for Chemistry, 1951*

LOUIS SHORES, *Ph.D., Dean of the Library School, Florida State University; Author and Authority on Reference Materials*

NILA BANTON SMITH, *Ph.B., Ph.D., Professor of Education and Director of The Reading Institute, New York University*

BRYAN SWAN, *M.S., Teacher of Physical Science, University of Chicago Laboratory Schools; Author*

SAMUEL TERRIEN, *S.T.M., Th.D., Auburn Professor of the Old Testament, Union Theological Seminary*

JESSIE TODD, *M.A., Formerly of the Art Department, University of Chicago; Art Lecturer; Contributor to Art Magazines*

LLOYD B. URDAL, *Ph.D., Assistant Professor, School of Education, State College of Washington*

JANE WERNER WATSON, *B.A., Editor and Author of More Than a Hundred Golden Books*

WILLIAM S. WEICHERT, *M.S., Supervisor of Science, Oakland (Calif.) Public Schools*

PAUL A. WITTY, *Ph.D., Professor of Education, Northwestern University; Specialist on Gifted Children*

STAFF

ROBERT D. BEZUCHA, *Project Director;* NORMAN F. GUESS, *Editorial Director;* R. JAMES ERTEL, *Managing Editor;* PAULINE NORTON, *Assistant Project Director;* ALICE F. MARTIN, *Associate Editor. Staff Editors:* GENEVIEVE CURLEY, JOAN FALK, HESTER GELB, RICHARD D. HARKINS.

THE GOLDEN BOOK ENCYCLOPEDIA

VOLUME IV—CHALK TO CZECHOSLOVAKIA

In Sixteen Accurate, Fact-filled Volumes Dramatically Illustrated
with More Than 6,000 Color Pictures

THE ONLY ENCYCLOPEDIA FOR YOUNG GRADE-SCHOOL CHILDREN

ACCURATE AND AUTHORITATIVE

ENTERTAININGLY WRITTEN AND ILLUSTRATED TO
MAKE LEARNING AN ADVENTURE

by Bertha Morris Parker

*Formerly of the Laboratory Schools, University of Chicago
Research Associate, Chicago Natural History Museum*

GOLDEN PRESS · NEW YORK

CHALK Countless millions of tiny animals too small to be seen without a microscope live in the sea. Some of them have the long name of foraminifera (fo ram i NIF er a). Under a microscope these tiny animals look like jewels. Each one has a shell which it has made for itself.

There are different kinds of foraminifera. They do not all make their shells of the same material. But a great many of them make their shells out of lime from the water. When these animals die, their shells are left behind and fall to the bottom of the water.

These little animals have lived on the earth for many millions of years. In some places long ago they lived in such numbers that their shells made a layer hundreds of feet thick on the floor of the sea. Then the bottom of the sea became dry land. The layer of shells became a layer of white rock. This white rock is a kind of limestone that we call chalk.

The famous white cliffs at Dover in England are made of chalk. There are layers of chalk in Kansas and other parts of the United States that are far away from the sea. These chalk layers show there were once seas where there are great areas of dry land today.

Chalk is used in making putty and paint. It is used in tooth powders and soft polishing powders. Some cement is made of it. Many farmers use it as a fertilizer.

But to many people the word "chalk" means only crayons for writing on blackboards. Long ago people found out that chalk is so soft that it can be used to write with. And for many years almost all blackboard crayons were made of it. Now many are made of other materials. But what fun to think, as we do an arithmetic problem on the blackboard, that we may be writing with the shells of little animals that lived millions of years ago. (See ROCKS.)

CHARIOT A circus sometimes ends with a chariot race. The chariots are two-wheeled carts without backs. Each one is pulled by either two or four horses. The drivers stand up, for there are no seats.

No one sees chariots now except in a circus or museum. But once they were used a great deal. Chariots were the very first wheeled vehicles. They were used in Babylonia as long ago as 2500 B.C. Ancient pictures show chariots drawn by donkeys.

Thundering chariot races were held in the Roman Coliseum nearly 2,000 years ago.

More than 3,500 years ago Egypt was conquered by people from Asia. The Egyptian soldiers fought on foot. The enemy rushed on them in chariots drawn by horses. The Egyptians had never seen horses or chariots before. In time the Egyptians drove out their conquerors. But they kept the idea of using chariots in war.

In ancient times chariots were used in processions, too. There were also chariot races. The book *Ben-Hur* tells a thrilling story of a Roman chariot race.

The Greeks and Romans thought that their gods sometimes rode in chariots. The sun moved from east to west, they believed, because the god of the sun drove across the sky each day in a chariot of gold.

Charlemagne Being Crowned Emperor

CHARLEMAGNE (SHAR le mane) (742-814) The name Charlemagne means "Charles the Great." It is one of the few great names that have come down to us from the Dark Ages.

When he was 26 years old, Charlemagne became the king of the Franks. He fought many battles to make his kingdom larger, and to spread Christianity, too. The Pope was grateful. On Christmas Day in the year 800 the Pope crowned Charlemagne as "Emperor of the Holy Roman Empire."

As emperor, Charlemagne did many things for his people. He was always ready to hear their troubles and to right them if he could. Above all, he did much to interest

his people in learning. He started schools, one of them in his own palace. Some of the boys who came to school were sons of rich nobles. They thought that they did not have to study. Charlemagne saw to it that they changed their minds.

Charlemagne could read, but he could not write. He kept a tablet under his pillow so that he could practice writing whenever he could not sleep.

Many stories about Charlemagne and his warriors were written down 1,000 years ago. They are some of the first stories ever written in French. (See DARK AGES; FRANCE; MIDDLE AGES; ROLAND.)

CHEESE An Arab once filled a pouch made from a calf's stomach with fresh milk and started on a long journey across a hot desert. With each step the pouch of milk swung from side to side. When the Arab stopped to drink from the pouch, the milk was no longer sweet nor was it liquid.

Instead, it was a solid mass which tasted quite different from anything the Arab had ever eaten.

This is only a story, but it shows how cheese may have first been made. We know that rennet, which is important in the digestion of food, is found in the stomachs of many animals. We know, too, that rennet will turn milk to cheese.

Cheese is the solid part of milk. It is mostly fat and protein. Cheese makers, by adding rennet or by letting bacteria sour the milk, make the solids of the milk come together in curds. The liquid part, or whey, is drained off.

There are many kinds of cheese. The kind is determined by the kind of milk used and by what is done to the curds. Cow's milk, sheep's milk, camel's milk, mare's milk, or goat's milk may be used. Some cheeses are allowed to ripen much longer than others. Some have special kinds of mold or bacteria added to give the cheese a special flavor.

Cheese may be hard, semihard, or soft. Swiss cheese is hard, Limburger is semihard, and Philadelphia cream cheese is soft.

Roquefort cheese is called "the king of cheeses." It was first made in Roquefort, France. It is a white cheese streaked with blue-green. The blue-green is a mold growing in the cheese. Holes are made in the cheese to let air reach the mold. In France, Roquefort cheese is made from sheep's milk. In the United States it is made from cow's milk and is called blue cheese. Some other famous cheeses are Cheddar cheese, first made in England, Edam or Gouda cheese from the Netherlands, and Mozzarella cheese from Italy.

Biggest of cheeses are the giant Swiss cheese wheels. Some weigh only a few pounds, but others may weigh a ton.

Cheese is a good food because it has in it almost everything that is in milk. People have lived for many months on a diet of cheese, brown bread, and fruit. (See FOODS; MILK; VITAMINS.)

CHEESES OF THE WORLD

Roquefort
France

Edam
Holland

Swiss
Switzerland

Mozzarella
Italy

American Cheddar
United States

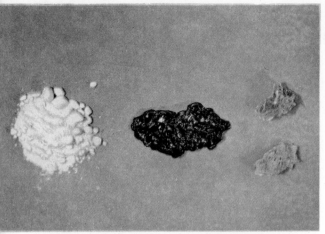

Sulfur does not always look the same.

CHEMISTRY For many hundreds of years people have been curious about what things are made of. It has not been enough for them to know that a house is made of bricks. "What are the bricks made of?" they ask. Finding that they are made of clay is not enough. "What is clay made of?" they want to know. Such curiosity led to the science of chemistry. Chemistry is the study of what things are made of.

Chemists have discovered that everything in the world is made of only about 100 simple substances. They call these simple substances elements.

But chemists do much more than tear substances apart to find out what elements are in them. They explain chemical changes, too. And they find ways of producing useful new substances.

A change is a chemical change when the materials at the end are different from those in the beginning. A baby drops his cup of milk. The china cup breaks, and the milk spills over the floor. The cup is ruined. But the china in it is still china. The milk is ruined, too, but it is still milk. A piece of paper falls into the fireplace by mistake and catches on fire. The paper is ruined. But the change in it is not like the change in the milk and the china. The paper is no longer paper. In place of the paper there are a few ashes and some invisible gases that escape into the air. Burning is a chemical change.

Chemical changes are going on around us all the time. Iron rusts. The color in cloth fades. Milk sours. Apples rot. Green plants make food out of materials from the air and the ground. All these are chemical changes.

Chemical changes are also going on inside our bodies every minute that we live. Some of the food we eat is being made over into muscle and blood and bone. Some of it is being slowly burned up so that we have energy enough to work and play.

Heat brings about some chemical changes. Heat, for instance, helps us get iron away from substances it is joined with

An Early Chemist in His Laboratory

CHEMISTRY IN EVERYDAY LIFE

From COAL, chemists get dyes to color WOOL and SILK and to make INK, and oils that go into paints for WOOD. SOFT DRINKS bubble with carbon dioxide gas. MILK contains the important chemical element, calcium, needed by our bodies. The golden color of BUTTER comes from a chemical dye. The chemist's "recipe" for SUGAR is $C_{12}H_{22}O_{11}$. It contains carbon, hydrogen, and oxygen. METALS are purified by smelting, which is a chemical process. Chemists have found that CLAY is a source of aluminum. Our refrigerators make ICE CUBES by using freon, an important product of chemistry.

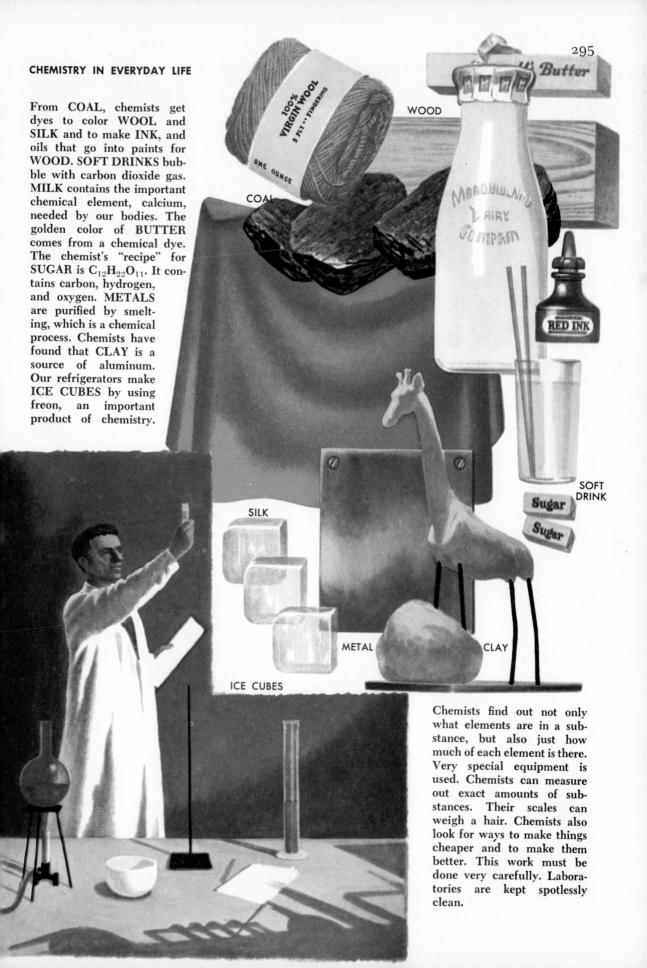

WOOD

COAL

RED INK

SOFT DRINK

Sugar

Sugar

SILK

METAL

CLAY

ICE CUBES

Chemists find out not only what elements are in a substance, but also just how much of each element is there. Very special equipment is used. Chemists can measure out exact amounts of substances. Their scales can weigh a hair. Chemists also look for ways to make things cheaper and to make them better. This work must be done very carefully. Laboratories are kept spotlessly clean.

THE CHEMIST'S LABORATORY

in iron ore. Light brings about some chemical changes. Some of these changes make it possible for us to take photographs. Electricity brings about chemical changes, too. One of these changes makes it possible for us to put a thin coat of silver on knives and forks and spoons.

Some chemical changes are very helpful. Others do harm. As soon as a chemist finds out what causes a chemical change, he can plan ways of starting it or preventing it. Chemists have found out, for instance, that

when iron rusts the iron joins with oxygen in the air to form iron rust. They have found, too, that iron does not rust unless there is some water present. Knowing what causes iron to rust has let chemists work out ways of keeping iron from rusting. One way is to keep the iron dry. Another way is to paint it so that the iron and the air do not come together.

Knowing what things are made of helps chemists put elements together to make new materials—such materials as nylon and cellophane. It also helps them find new ways to make materials they already know about—such things as paints and diamonds, dyes, and drugs. Suppose, for example, a drug is found that cures a certain disease. Suppose, too, that this drug comes from a rare plant that is very expensive and hard to get. Chemists now come into the picture. They tear the drug apart to see what it is made of. Then they try to make it from materials they can get easily. Usually they succeed.

Once all the chemists were in schools and colleges. Now, many of the big manufacturing companies have chemists working for them. Many of the boys and girls of today are sure to grow up to be chemists. (See COAL TAR; COMPOUNDS; DRUGS; ELEMENTS; NYLON; PLASTICS.)

CHEWING GUM Long ago people in different parts of the world discovered that some trees produce a gum which can be chewed and chewed without disappearing. But chewing gum as we know it was first made in the United States.

At first the gum from black spruce trees was used. It was purified and sweetened. Later the gum from various other trees was tried, and a cheap chewing gum was made from paraffin. Today most chewing gum is made from chicle. Chicle is the sap of the sapodilla tree, which grows in Central and South America. Every year thousands of tons of chicle for chewing gum are shipped to the United States.

The people of the United States spend millions of dollars a year for chewing gum. Big fortunes have been made by some of its manufacturers.

Black Spruce

HOW GUM IS MADE

Chiclero Slashing the Chicle Tree

Chicle Milk

Transportation of Milk in Canvas Bags

Boiling Chicle Milk

Hot Chicle Being Molded

Chicle Bricks Cooling

Chewing Gum Factory

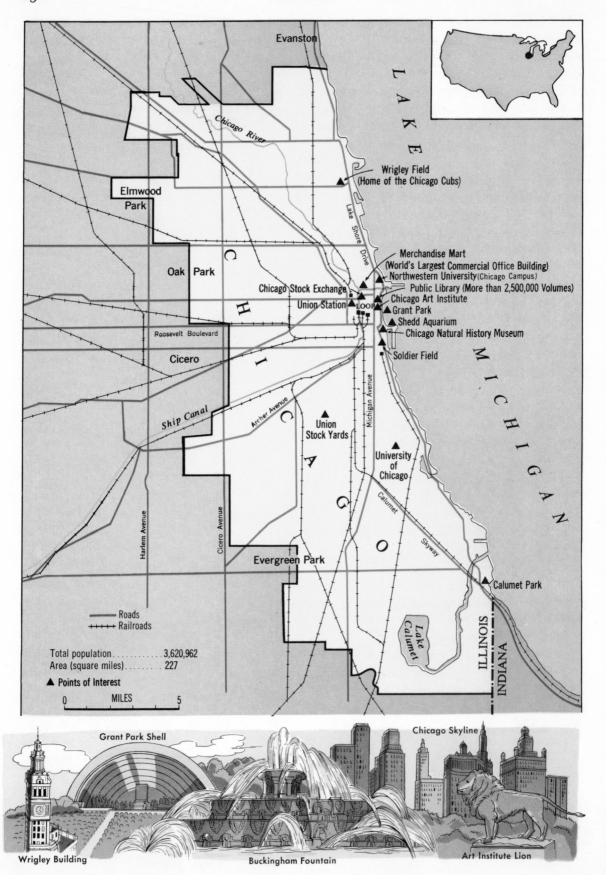

Evanston

Chicago River

L A K E

Wrigley Field
(Home of the Chicago Cubs)

Elmwood
Park

Lake Shore Drive

Oak Park

Merchandise Mart
(World's Largest Commercial Office Building)
Northwestern University (Chicago Campus)
Public Library (More than 2,500,000 Volumes)

Chicago Stock Exchange

C H I C A G O

Chicago Art Institute

Union Station   LOOP   Grant Park

Shedd Aquarium

Chicago Natural History Museum

Roosevelt Boulevard

Cicero

Michigan Avenue

Soldier Field

M I C H I G A N

Ship Canal

Archer Avenue

Union
Stock Yards

University
of
Chicago

Calumet

Skyway

Harlem Avenue

Cicero Avenue

Evergreen Park

Calumet Park

Lake
Calumet

ILLINOIS

INDIANA

Roads
Railroads

Total population............ 3,620,962
Area (square miles).......... 227

▲ Points of Interest

0   MILES   5

Grant Park Shell

Chicago Skyline

Wrigley Building

Buckingham Fountain

Art Institute Lion

CHICAGO The story of Chicago begins in 1830. In that year the little village of Chicago was laid out around Fort Dearborn, a small fort near the southern end of Lake Michigan. Now this small village has become one of the world's ten largest cities. It is the second-largest city in the United States. Only New York is larger.

Chicago is only about half as big as New York, but New York is 200 years older. It is not quite half as big as London, but London has had 2,000 years to grow in.

Railroads, meat, and steel help explain why Chicago has grown so fast. The city is the greatest railroad center, one of the greatest meat-packing centers, and one of the leading steel producing centers of the entire world.

The shortest land routes from the thickly settled northeastern part of the United States to much of the West pass along the southern end of Lake Michigan. At Chicago, those land routes meet lake routes. Level land stretches for many miles east, south, and west from the southern end of the lake. Building roads and railroads on this level land was fairly easy.

Coal from the south and east, and iron ore from the iron mines near Lake Superior found an easy meeting place in Chicago. The iron ore could be brought rather cheaply down the lakes in big ore boats. The coal could be brought on the railroads in rather short hauls. Coal and iron are needed for making steel. Huge steel mills grew up in and near Chicago.

Chicago is near the great Corn Belt. It is within easy reach by railroad of the Great Plains. Cattle, hogs, and sheep could easily be shipped from Corn Belt farms and Great Plains ranches to the city. Meat-packing was soon one of Chicago's chief industries.

With steel at hand and with much level land round about, it is not surprising that many factories, such as those that make farming machinery, were started in Chicago. Nearness to the Corn Belt and to the western wheat lands gave the city a big advantage as a grain trading center. Some factories were attracted to the city by the big supply of fresh water in the lake.

Chicago had a serious setback in 1871. A great fire burned down a large part of the city. But the fire may have been a help in the end. For the buildings built to take the place of those that were burned were better than the old ones.

Most visitors to Chicago today are eager to see the stockyards and the great steel mills. But there is much else for them to see: the wonderful Outer Drive along the shore of Lake Michigan; many boulevards and parks; two big zoos; some of the finest museums in the world; the business center, or Loop, with tall skyscrapers, great department stores, and huge hotels; several famous universities; the world's largest commercial office building (the Merchandise Mart); and many miles of beautiful homes.

Many visitors come and go by automobile or bus on the broad skyway or "pike," that links Chicago with the Atlantic seaboard. Other great highways now link the city with many places. And in Chicago is Midway Airport, the busiest airport in the world. The newer, larger Chicago International Airport is a very busy one, too.

Now more than 40 railroads carry freight and passengers to and from the city. The city has become more and more important as a port, too. A canal-river waterway linking Lake Michigan with the Gulf of Mexico has helped it to do so. So has the new St. Lawrence Seaway. This seaway permits large ocean-going vessels to reach Chicago. Clearly, Chicago is a great center of transport by rail, road, river, canal, lake, ocean, and air.

Chicago is nicknamed the Windy City. There are some days when the city deserves this nickname, but they do not come very often. The lake helps make Chicago's climate a pleasant one much of the time. (See CORN BELT; ILLINOIS; IRON AND STEEL; MEAT AND MEAT-PACKING; ST. LAWRENCE RIVER.)

CHILE One country of South America stretches for more than 2,600 miles along the Pacific Ocean. This country is Chile. Chile is far longer than any other country of South America. But it is not the largest country of that continent, for it is very narrow. It is not as much as 250 miles wide anywhere. People often call it South America's "shoestring" country.

Chile is south of the equator. So its northern part is its warmest part and its southern part is its coolest part. In Chile it is summer when it is winter in the United States. And June, July, and August are winter months in Chile.

Much of Chile is mountainous. Most of its eastern boundary is in the very high Andes Mountains, which stretch along the whole Pacific coast of South America.

But there is lowland, too. Most of the Chileans live in a great north-south valley in the central part of the country.

Valparaiso is the gateway to this valley from the sea. The city's name means "vale of paradise." The central valley *is* a beautiful region. Its climate is like the climate of California. Much of the land is in well-kept farms. There are wheat fields, vineyards, fruit and olive orchards, and sheep and cattle pastures.

Santiago, the capital of Chile, is in the central valley. It is the fourth-largest city of South America. No capital in the world has more beautiful surroundings. The snowy peaks of the Andes tower to the east. There are hills to the west. Many tourists visit Santiago because of its beauty. Its great avenue, Alameda, is one of the world's most famous streets.

A great deal of Chile is not at all like the central valley. In the highland north of the central valley there is a vast desert. It is by no means a paradise. In places in this desert, years go by without a drop of rain. Visitors talk about the naked ground there. Not even the stoutest cactus plants can grow in that dry soil.

But strangely enough, much of Chile's wealth is in this desert. For here there are

El Tronador (Volcano)

Grapes

Farmhouse

Huaso (Cowboy)

Pangue Plant

great beds of rock that contain nitrate of soda. Nitrate of soda is an important kind of fertilizer. Every year Chile sells millions of dollars' worth of this fertilizer to other lands. Besides, in producing nitrate of soda, iodine is also produced. More than half of all the iodine used in the world comes from Chile.

In Chile's northern desert there are also great copper mines. The copper deposit there is thought to be the richest copper deposit in the whole world. Chile's copper is worth even more than its nitrate. There are deposits of iron and borax and salt in the desert region, too.

South of the great central valley the mountains come close to the coast. This part of Chile is cool, and there is much rain. It is a land of many forests and many sheep ranches. The biggest city of southern Chile is Punta Arenas. It is farther south than any other city in the world.

About a twentieth of all the people of Chile are pure Indian. About a fourth of the people are white. They are mostly Spanish or German or English. The others are part Indian and part Spanish. Their ancestors were Indians who were living in the land when Columbus discovered America, and Spaniards who conquered that part of the New World. (See ANDES; CAPE HORN; SOUTH AMERICA.)

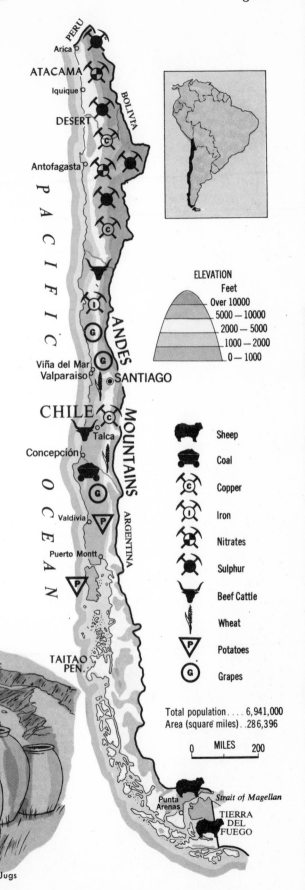

ELEVATION
Feet
Over 10000
5000 — 10000
2000 — 5000
1000 — 2000
0 — 1000

Sheep
Coal
Copper
Iron
Nitrates
Sulphur
Beef Cattle
Wheat
Potatoes
Grapes

Total population.... 6,941,000
Area (square miles)..286,396

0   MILES   200

Copper Mining

Llama

NITRATES

Giant Squash   Wine Jugs

The Great Wall of China is 1,500 miles long.

CHINA The Chinese outnumber the people of any other country. There are about 600 million Chinese. One out of every five people in the world is Chinese.

In size, China is as big as all Europe. It is in southeastern Asia. It stretches westward from the Pacific Ocean for more than 2,000 miles. Its northernmost town is farther north than Quebec, Canada. But its southern coast is as far south as Cuba. The only country larger than China is the Soviet Union.

The Chinese were among the early peoples to build a great civilization. It is thought that 3,000 years ago they were already irrigating little farms, raising silkworms, and weaving silk cloth. They were traveling in two-wheeled carts, writing with picturelike signs, and building cities. By 2,000 years ago, they had built the early Chinese Empire.

The Great Wall, 1,500 miles long, was built by the Chinese to shut out invading tribes from the north. Great deserts and mountain ranges to the west and the Pacific Ocean to the east gave China other protection. Distances between China and other early civilized countries were great. So it is not surprising that until recent times the Chinese knew little about other peoples. Long before those times, the Chinese had invented ways of living all their own.

Writing with a brush and eating with chopsticks are Chinese customs that seem odd to Western peoples. But some things the Chinese invented are now used every-where. Printing is one of them. Today, beautiful things the Chinese have made of silk, paper, porcelain, bronze, jade, and the like are sold in shops in many lands. And in China there now are airports, railroads, and modern factories besides the many very old kinds of things.

Most of the people in China live in the southeastern part of that huge country. Few of them live in western China. The west is a land of plateaus and mountains. And it gets little rain. Eastern China has fewer mountains and more rain. The northern, cooler part of it is called Manchuria. It has many more people than there are in the west. More than a million of them live in its largest city, Mukden.

At least a sixth of the world's people live in southeastern China. Millions of them are in its many big cities. The population of Shanghai is about 7,000,000. Canton, Tientsin, and Peiping are cities of more than 1,000,000 people. But most of the people in southeastern China live in its thousands of farm villages.

China has great mineral riches. Among them are coal and iron. But it often is said that its greatest riches are the Hwang Ho, Yangtze, and Si rivers in southeastern China and the farmland in and near their valleys and deltas.

In spite of those rich farmlands, China's farmers are poor. They need many times as much farmland as they have. It is very hard to make even a bare living from a farm of only two or three acres.

The chief crop in the southern half of southeastern China is rice. It is raised in fields that can be flooded. The rice fields lie on the valley floors and climb the hills on stairways of terraces built by the farmers. Winters are warm, and two crops of rice are grown each year.

Farther north, between the Yangtze and Hwang Ho rivers, land is less hilly. Winters are not warm. From the air, the huge plain crossed by the Hwang Ho River looks like an immense carpet of fields of wheat, mil-

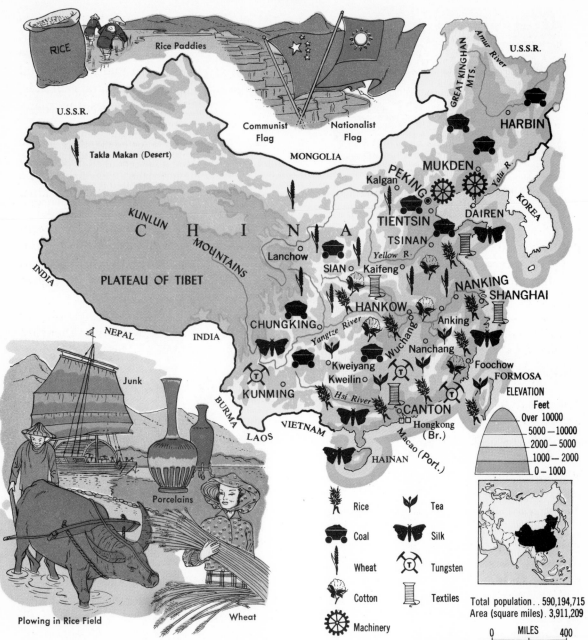

RICE

Rice Paddies

U.S.S.R.

Takla Makan (Desert)

Communist
Flag

Nationalist
Flag

MONGOLIA

Amur River

U.S.S.R.

GREAT KINGHAN MTS.

HARBIN

MUKDEN

PEKING
Kalgan

TIENTSIN

DAIREN

KOREA

Yalu R.

TSINAN

Yellow R.

KUNLUN
MOUNTAINS

C H I N A

Lanchow

SIAN   Kaifeng

NANKING
SHANGHAI

PLATEAU OF TIBET

HANKOW

CHUNGKING

Yangtze River

Wuchang

Anking

Nanchang

INDIA

NEPAL

INDIA

Junk

Kweiyang
Kweilin

Foochow

FORMOSA

ELEVATION
Feet
Over 10000
5000 — 10000
2000 — 5000
1000 — 2000
0 — 1000

BURMA

Hsi River

KUNMING

CANTON

Hongkong
(Br.)

Macao (Port.)

VIETNAM

LAOS

Porcelains

HAINAN

Rice   Tea

Coal   Silk

Wheat   Tungsten

Cotton   Textiles

Machinery

Total population . . 590,194,715
Area (square miles) . 3,911,209

0   MILES   400

Plowing in Rice Field   Wheat

let, and cotton. Dark-green dots in the carpet are clusters of trees in the mud-walled
farm villages. In Manchuria the winters
are very cold. The chief crops are millet
and soybeans.

Today the government in control of all
the mainland of China is bringing about a
big change in farming. In 1912 the Chinese
set up a new government, a republic. Chinese Communists got control in 1949, set
up a communist government, and made

Peiping their capital. Much land the farmers had owned is now in state farms man-
aged by the government. Chinese foes of
the communists set up a Chinese government in the Chinese island of Taiwan, or
Formosa. So China has two governments.
Whether old, independent China will con-
tinue to be under the control of communists is one of the world's important ques-
tions. (See HISTORY; HWANG HO;
MARCO POLO; SHANGHAI.)

The earliest pottery was shaped by hand.

CHINA AND POTTERY A person can cup his hands and dip up water from a stream to drink. But he must go to the stream to get a drink in this way. A piece of meat can be roasted on a stick over a bonfire. But most vegetables cannot be cooked on a stick. Apples can be stored by piling them up in some corner. But honey cannot be stored in that way. Very long ago our ancestors felt the need of containers for water and food. And very long ago they found that it was possible to form wet clay into useful bowls and jars of various shapes and sizes.

We still use clay for making bowls and jars used in cooking and storing food. We use it for plates and cups and saucers. We use it for vases and beautiful figures. All these things made of clay are called pottery or china. China is really just a special

Men learned to make beautiful pottery.

kind of pottery. It is rather glassy, and it is made in such a way that some light can shine through it. It got its name "china" because the Chinese first found out how to make it. They guarded their secret from the rest of the world for hundreds of years. Another name for china is porcelain.

The first clay vessels were probably dried in the sun. Then people found out that clay vessels baked in a fire were much better. In time they learned to put on a waterproof glaze.

Probably the discovery of how to make pottery was made many times in many different places. At least pottery has been

Pueblo Indians knew how to make painted pottery.

found in the ruins of ancient villages in many different parts of the world. Of course, most of this pottery is broken. But even so it tells scientists a great deal about the people who lived where the ruins are.

The first potters were interested mostly in making their pottery useful. Then they became interested in making it beautiful, too. Twenty-five hundred years ago the Greeks made vases as lovely as any that have ever been made.

Making a piece of china or pottery is not at all simple. Good clay for pottery making must be found. Then there are five steps: mixing, shaping, firing, glazing, and decorating. The last three steps do not always come in the same order.

Mixing is always the first step. The clay must be mixed with water. Perhaps some other materials must be added. For a special kind of china called bone china, for instance, ashes from bones must be mixed with the clay and water. The mixture may be thin enough to be poured. It may be as thick as bread dough.

Shaping is always the second step. In the earliest days of pottery all of it was shaped by hand. The picture of pottery making long ago shows the women doing the shaping with only their hands. But for several thousand years people have used the potter's wheel for shaping pottery. Wheel-made pottery dating back more than 4,500 years has been found in the ruins of ancient cities in the Near East.

A potter's wheel lets the potter turn the clay round and round as he shapes it. He presses his thumbs and fingers into the clay in just the right places to push it into the shape he wants.

Another way to shape pottery is to use a mold. Much of the pottery of today is made with molds.

Firing means baking in an oven, or kiln. A piece of pottery is fired as soon as it is shaped. It is fired at least once more and perhaps several times. The last firing is always the last step.

A glaze is a substance that hardens into a thin layer of glass. It can be given beautiful colors. A piece of pottery must be fired after it has been coated with a glaze. It may sometimes be given more than one layer of glaze.

Ancient Greek Jug

Chinese Vase

Roman Wine Jug

Potter's Wheel

California Indian Jug

Chinese Dish

Ancient Egyptian Bottle

New Mexico Indian Dish and Jar

There are several ways of decorating a piece of pottery. A design may be pressed into the soft clay before the first firing. It may be put on by adding extra clay before the first firing. It may be painted on before glazing. It may be painted on after the first glazing. The only decoration on a piece of pottery may be the glaze itself.

None of these ways of decorating pottery is new. Pottery with painted designs was being made even before the use of the potter's wheel. Later, in ancient Athens, vessels of all shapes and sizes were decorated with beautiful paintings. Some showed Greek gods and heroes. Others showed scenes from everyday life. Both the potters and the painters were proud of their work and often signed the pieces.

Most of the pictures here show pottery of long ago. Much beautiful pottery is being made today, too. Many places in the world are famous for their pottery.

Ancient Greek Vase

Pottery from the Bible Lands

The pearl-gray chinchilla fur is very valuable.

CHINCHILLA The chinchilla is one of the rodents—the gnawing mammals. It is therefore a cousin of the rats, mice, squirrels, and chipmunks. Its home is in the mountains of South America.

There are not many wild chinchillas left. Most of them have been killed for their beautiful fur, which is a pearly gray and is very thick and soft. Chinchillas are now raised on farms just as mink and foxes are.

Wild chinchillas are shy little creatures. They feed chiefly at dusk. If anything disturbs them, they pop into their holes among the rocks. But they soon stick their heads out to see what is going on.

Like other rodents, chinchillas eat plants. They eat grasses, grains, fruits, and roots. When they have found something to eat they hold it in their front paws and nibble it just as squirrels and chipmunks do. (See FURS; RODENTS.)

CHLORINE Back in 1774 a Swedish scientist heated a mixture of chemicals. Out of the mixture bubbled a greenish-yellow gas that had a suffocating odor. The scientist, Karl Wilhelm Scheele, thought he had made a new gas containing oxygen. Years later another scientist proved that Scheele had discovered chlorine.

Chlorine is one of the simple substances called elements. In nature it is always joined with at least one other element. It is, we say, always in a compound. Salt is a compound made of chlorine and sodium.

Although chlorine is a gas, it can be changed to a liquid. Great amounts of it are sold in liquid form.

Chlorine is poisonous to breathe. In World War I it was used as a poison gas. Fortunately, it is poisonous to germs, too. Small amounts of it are dissolved in the water of swimming pools to kill germs. Many large cities use it to purify their drinking water, too.

Chlorine is also used in bleaching solutions. These solutions help keep white cottons and linens white during washings.

From their names it is easy to guess that carbon tetrachloride and chloroform have chlorine in them. Carbon tetrachloride can be used to put out fires. It is also a good cleaning fluid. Chloroform is sometimes used in hospitals as an anesthetic.

Special chemicals are needed to produce the white smoke for skywriting. These special chemicals are chlorine compounds. (See COMPOUNDS; ELEMENTS.)

CHOCOLATE AND COCOA Both chocolate and cocoa are made from the seeds of the cacao tree. The scientific name of this tree is *Theobroma*. It means "food for the gods." The famous Swedish botanist Linnaeus (li NEE us) gave it this name after tasting chocolate for the first time. Many people today like chocolate and cocoa so much that they would agree that the cacao tree deserves its name.

Cacao trees can be raised only near the equator. They need much warmth. The trees grow to be about 20 feet tall. They have small leathery leaves and pink blossoms. Many of the pink blossoms fall off, but some stay on and grow into seed pods. Usually there are about 20 pods on a tree. A pod may be more than 12 inches long. The seeds in it are almond-shaped.

When the seed pods are ripe, they are cut from the tree and allowed to dry for a few hours. The pulp and seeds are then scooped out of the pods. After several days

The pulp and seeds are removed from the pod.

the pulp ferments and the seeds, or beans, separate from it. The beans are then washed, dried, and shipped to factories. After roasting, the thin skins of the beans are cracked off and blown away. The kernels, or "nibs," are left. Chocolate is made by grinding the nibs between hot rollers. Sometimes sugar is added. For cocoa, the fat in the chocolate is removed. This fat, or cocoa butter, is not thrown away. It is used in candy, ointments, and soaps.

When the Spanish explorer Cortés came to Mexico, he found the people there using a drink they called chocolate. It was highly spiced and strong with pepper. Cortés and his men learned to drink it. But not till the Spaniards added sugar instead of pepper did they like chocolate. By 1600 "chocolate" had reached Europe. A hundred years later the English had learned to make a very good drink of chocolate by using milk instead of water.

Today tons of chocolate and cocoa are used. Not only drinks, but candies, cakes, puddings, and pies are flavored with it.

The cacao tree is an American plant. It still grows wild in the northern part of South America. We know it was being cultivated in Mexico and Central America in the time of Cortés. Later Brazil and other countries of South America began to cultivate it. Today most of the world's supply comes from Brazil and tropical Africa.

Jesus Speaking to the Multitude

CHRISTIANITY One of the world's great religions is Christianity. It is the religion of about three-quarters of a billion people. More people follow Christianity than any other religion of the world. Christianity is built on the work of Jesus Christ. Jesus lived nearly 2,000 years ago. Christianity, then, is nearly 2,000 years old.

Jesus told his followers that they should follow these two important commandments above all else:

Thou shalt love the Lord with all thy heart and with all thy soul.

Thou shalt love thy neighbor as thyself.

After Jesus rose from the dead, his disciples had such faith in him that they became fearless preachers and spread his teachings. But Paul, who was not one of the 12 disciples, did more than anyone else to spread Christianity in its early days. He

Canterbury Cathedral in England

traveled over many lands and founded churches in many places.

At first Christians were badly treated. The Jews treated them badly because the Jews had not accepted Jesus as their religious leader. The Romans treated them badly, too. The early Christians were sometimes forced to fight lions and other wild animals while Romans watched the sport.

But Christianity did not die. Instead, it grew stronger. During the Middle Ages it had a great hold on the people of Europe. They built huge cathedrals in which to worship. Their church was more important to them than their king or their country.

Many different ideas arose of how Christ should be worshiped. There came to be

Jesus Blessing a Little Child

many different branches of Christianity that had different forms of worship. There are still many branches today.

The Bible is the sacred book of all Christians. In it are the teachings of Christ which Christians try to follow. More copies of the Bible have been sold than of any other book ever written.

Jesus taught that every human being is important in the eyes of God. The idea that every human being is important is the idea back of letting people rule themselves. It is the idea back of democracy. (See BIBLE; CHRISTMAS; JESUS; RELIGIONS OF THE WORLD; TEN COMMANDMENTS; TWELVE DISCIPLES.)

CHRISTMAS The 25th of December is one of our happiest holidays. It is the day we celebrate as the birthday of Jesus. We call it Christmas.

At first several different days were celebrated as the day when Jesus was born. December 25 is the day that most Christians finally agreed to call his birthday.

The name Christmas is short for "Christ's Mass." A Mass is a kind of church service. Christmas is a religious festival. There are special Christmas services in Christian churches all over the world. But many of the festivities of Christmas do not have anything to do with religion.

The idea of gifts at Christmas time may have come from the story of the three Wise Men. In some countries Christmas presents are not given until January 6, or Twelfth Night, the time when the Wise Men brought gifts to the baby Jesus. But many people think that the idea of Christmas gifts came from an old Roman custom. December 21 is the shortest day of the year. Right after that time days begin getting longer. The people of long ago were very happy when the days began getting longer. They thought of the return of longer days as the birthday of the sun. Christmas comes at just about the time the Romans were exchanging gifts to celebrate the lengthening of day. Exchanging gifts and sending Christmas cards are modern ways of making the Christmas season merry.

Decorating with holly, mistletoe, and evergreens goes back to an early custom in northern Europe. The people there used the decorations we now call Christmas greens to celebrate the time when days grow longer.

Burning a great Yule log is another custom that grew up in northern Europe as a part of the midwinter celebration. Bringing in the Yule log was a joyous ceremony in old England. The Yule log is still important in many places.

The idea of Christmas trees came from Germany. Now it has spread to many other countries throughout the world.

A little manger scene may take the place of a Christmas tree in many lands. The scene shows the baby Jesus cradled in a manger. Mary and Joseph are watching over him. Standing near are several animals—some sheep, perhaps, and a donkey. There may be a shepherd or two. The French people call a scene of this kind a crèche (KRAYSH).

The name "Santa Claus" comes from "Saint Nicholas." St. Nicholas is considered the special friend of children. Dutch children put wooden shoes in front of the fireplace for St. Nicholas to fill the night before his feast day, December 6. In America the idea of a saint changed to the idea of a jolly, fat man dressed in red who lives at the North Pole and rides in a sleigh drawn by reindeer. American children hang up their stockings on Christmas Eve and hope that Santa Claus will fill them with toys and good things to eat.

In many countries groups of children go about singing Christmas carols. There are many beautiful carols.

In many parts of the world Christmas is likely to be a time of ice and snow. People like a "White Christmas." But in warmer regions there is no snow at Christmas time. South of the equator December comes in summer. Christmas day may be a hot summer day, and Christmas dinner may be a picnic on the beach.

Ores of Chromium

Chromium is used for trim on modern cars.

CHROMIUM Many people know what chromium looks like, for the bright metal trimming on automobiles is plated with chromium. The plating is very thin, but it makes a pretty covering for the steel underneath and keeps it from rusting.

Chromium, however, would not be a very important metal if it were used just to trim automobiles. Really very little of all the chromium used goes for trimmings. Far more goes into making stainless steel.

The name "chromium" comes from the Greek word for "color." Chromium gives a beautiful color to many of the substances in which it is found. Rubies, emeralds, and some sapphires owe their color to the presence of chromium.

Chromium is never found pure. The people of ancient times did not know that there was such a metal.

One of the ores which contains chromium is called chromite. Chromite is useful as a lining for furnaces for making steel.

There is a great deal of chromium ore in the United States. But until World War II supplies were easier to get from other countries. Then, during the war, there was danger that the supplies might be shut off. Americans started mining their own chromium. Men blasted tunnels into the Beartooth Mountains in Montana and began digging away tons of ore. With this huge supply American manufacturers will probably never have to worry about needing chromium. (See ELEMENTS; METALS.)

CHURCHILL, SIR WINSTON LEONARD SPENCER (1874-) Few people in history have been outstanding in as many fields as Winston Churchill. He has won world fame as a war leader, writer, and public speaker.

Churchill's father was English—a descendant of the famous Duke of Marlborough. His mother was an American. When he was 21, Churchill joined the British Army and served for a time in India. In 1900, while working as a newspaper correspondent in the Boer War in Africa, he was captured. He made a daring escape and returned home a hero. In that same year he was elected to Parliament.

During World War I, Churchill held important positions in the British cabinet. In the years following the war his importance grew less. But before World War II began, Churchill again became prominent by warning about the danger from Hitler. When World War II started, Churchill was put in charge of the British Navy. Less than a year later he became Prime Minister.

It is as Prime Minister that Churchill is best known. He became the leader of his country in May, 1940. The following month, Italy joined Germany in the war against France and England. Within days France surrendered. Everyone thought England would soon be invaded. Churchill told his people they would have to expect "blood, toil, tears, and sweat." But he promised that England would never surrender.

Confidence and courage rang out in every speech Churchill made to his coun-

trymen. The English endured terrific bombings, but they fought back. Churchill did much to give his people the will and the spirit to carry on.

Churchill has written many books. In 1953 he won the Nobel prize for literature for his six-volume history of World War II. (See ENGLAND; WORLD WAR II.)

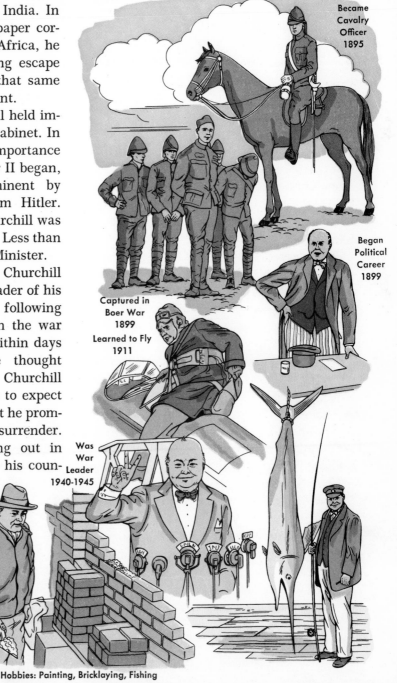

Became Cavalry Officer 1895

Captured in Boer War 1899

Learned to Fly 1911

Began Political Career 1899

Was War Leader 1940-1945

Hobbies: Painting, Bricklaying, Fishing

CIRCLES

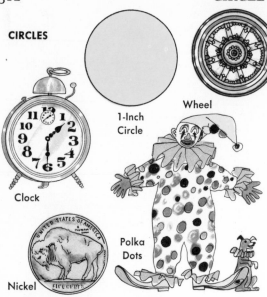

1-Inch Circle

Wheel

Clock

Polka Dots

Nickel

CIRCLE Put a dot on a piece of paper. Draw a line and make it curve so that it is always the same distance from the dot. The line will finally reach the place where it started. On the paper there will be a circle with the dot in the center. An easy way to draw a circle is to use a drawing tool called a compass. Every part of a perfect circle is exactly the same distance from the center. This distance is the radius.

Anyone hunting for circles will find them almost everywhere. Bracelets and rings are circles. So are wheels and tires. Polka dots are circles with their centers filled in. The faces of most clocks and watches are solid circles, too. The full moon is a solid circle as we see it in the sky.

The equator is an imaginary circle around the earth halfway between the South Pole and the North Pole. The center of this circle is deep inside the earth. The path of the earth around the sun is almost a circle.

The easiest way of telling how big a circle is, is to tell its diameter. The diameter of a circle is the distance across it through its center. The diameter of the equator is nearly 8,000 miles. It is 500,-000,000 times as great as the diameter of the yellow circle at the top of this page. (See MATHEMATICS.)

CIRCUS "The circus is coming to town" is good news to boys and girls everywhere. Perhaps the circus that comes is a small one. Perhaps it is "the greatest show on earth." No matter how big it is, it is sure to be fun.

The word "circus" is much like the word "circle." There is a good reason why. Every circus has one or more circles, or rings, where the performances go on. A big circus usually has three rings. But it may have as many as five.

The first circus we know anything about was in ancient Rome. The Roman circus was made up mostly of chariot races. But between races acrobats and horseback riders performed. After the fall of Rome there were no circuses for centuries. Then, about 200 years ago, small circuses began traveling about in England. The performers were acrobats and jugglers. They performed on the village greens.

The first circus in America was in Philadelphia in George Washington's time. Washington went once. Soon afterward there were circuses in many places. At first they were in open fields. Then tents began to be used.

P. T. Barnum did much to make circuses into the great shows they are now. He had many new ideas. In a circus today there are acrobats, trapeze performers, bareback

Most circuses have three rings and lots of action.

riders, and trained animals. There are special stunts high in the air—such stunts as walking a tightrope and riding a bicycle along a high wire. There are side shows outside the main tent and usually a menagerie of caged wild animals. And always there are clowns. A circus without clowns would not seem like a circus at all.

On circus day there used to be a parade in the morning. Elephants, cages of wild animals, bands, and riders on horseback made up most of the parade. It ended with a steam calliope (ka LI o pe) that played a tune. Now, in most towns, the old-fashioned circus parades have been given up. They interfere with heavy traffic, and they are very expensive.

Many people take part in circus performances. There are many more behind the scenes. Loading and unloading a circus is an enormous amount of work. Putting up the big tent with its seats is hard work, too. Besides all this, the circus people and the animals must be fed.

Late in the fall circuses go into winter quarters. New costumes and new acts must be made ready for the next season. Circus owners want people to keep on being glad when the circus comes to town. (See BANDS; BARNUM, P. T.; FAIRS.)

Stockholm, the largest city in Sweden, is a busy seaport.

CITIES There were many great cities in ancient times. Thebes, Babylon, Nineveh, Tyre, Damascus, Athens, Carthage, Byzantium, and Rome were a few of them. Their story is an important part of the story of civilization. Some of the cities of ancient times are still cities today. Others have been buried for centuries.

About 1,500 years ago barbarian tribes pushed their way into the great Roman Empire. They brought about its ruin. They burned down most of the cities. City life did not appeal to them. They were used to

Many old cities were walled in for protection.

roaming about from place to place. Europe remained a land of pastures and little villages for many years.

But after a dozen generations or so these barbarians settled down. There came to be great lords who lived in castles. Clusters of huts grew up in the shadow of the castle walls. The people were safer there. Great cathedrals were built, and many people came to live nearby. Castle and cathedral villages slowly grew into cities.

The wars called the Crusades helped make the cities of Europe grow. The knights who went to fight in the Holy Land saw that their way of living was not the only way. They wanted finer clothes, more comfortable homes, and more interesting foods. They wanted silks and spices and perfumes from the East. Merchants were needed. Bankers were needed, too, to arrange for the buying and selling of goods. The need for merchants and bankers was one reason for the growth of cities in Europe. It was easier for them to do business with one another if their places of business were near each other.

When European cities began to grow, there were no strong nations to keep law and order. Cities had to protect themselves from bands of robbers. They had to protect themselves, too, from neighboring nobles who wanted to conquer them. Many cities of the Middle Ages had walls around them. An old walled city is the heart of a number of cities of Europe today.

Early in the Middle Ages people raised most of their own food. They made their own clothes. They built their own houses. There was very little buying and selling. But along with wanting better homes and better things to wear and to eat, many people began making things to sell. They soon found that some things could be made better in factories than at home. The growth of factories helped cities grow.

Cities have not always been pleasant places to live. A person from a city of the Middle Ages would marvel at the smooth pavements, the bright street lights, and the hidden sewers of today's cities. He would be surprised not to see pigs rooting for garbage in the mud in the streets. He would be surprised, too, at all the care that cities now take to keep dangerous contagious diseases from spreading.

The invention of the steam engine and its use in factories gave a very big push to the growth of cities. So did the building of good roads and railroads.

Today there are about 75 cities that have more than a million people in them. These cities are scattered all over the world. Australia has the fewest large cities of all the continents—except, of course, Antarctica, which has no people at all. Asia, which has the world's largest population, has the greatest number of large cities.

It is not just by chance that big cities have grown up where they are. One city may be at a place where travel by land meets travel by sea. Perhaps another is near a big coal field or on a great river or in an area where water power is cheap. An important part of the story of every city is how it came to be where it is.

The list below names 10 of the world's very large cities.

CITY	COUNTRY	POPULATION
Tokyo	Japan	Over 8,000,000
London	England	" 8,000,000
New York	United States	" 7,000,000
Shanghai	China	" 7,000,000
Moscow	U.S.S.R.	" 4,000,000
Mexico City	Mexico	" 4,000,000
Peiping	China	" 4,000,000
Chicago	United States	" 3,000,000
Buenos Aires	Argentina	" 3,000,000
Berlin	Germany	" 3,000,000

Many of the world's biggest cities are ports that have become centers of trade.

A Roman's proudest boast was, "I am a Roman citizen."

CITIZENSHIP *The Man Without a Country,* by Edward Everett Hale, is the story of a man accused of treason. At his trial he said that he hoped he would never hear the name of his country again. The judge gave him his wish. For 55 years he was not allowed to set foot in his country or hear any news of it. He was not a citizen of any country. As he was dying, homesick and friendless, he begged to be taken back to his native land.

Most of us do not realize how important it is to be a citizen of a country. Every country helps its citizens in many ways. Back in the days of ancient Rome, a Roman's proudest boast was, "I am a Roman citizen." A country helps and protects its citizens even when they are in other lands.

Different countries have different ways of deciding who is a citizen. Being born in a country may make a person a citizen of that country. Having parents who are both citizens of the same country may make a child a citizen of that country no matter where he is born. Many citizens of the United States are naturalized citizens. They are immigrants who came from other countries and decided that they wished to become American citizens. The laws of the United States tell the steps a person must take to become naturalized.

Being a citizen of a country does not mean merely getting protection and help from its government. It also means that the citizen has duties to his country. He owes it to his country to obey its laws and to pay the taxes asked of him. He owes it to his country to fight for it if he is called on to do so.

If his country is a democracy, a citizen should take part in its government. He should try to find out what his country's problems are. He should show what he thinks should be done by voting for those who stand for what he believes. He should do his share in helping to make his country one of which all its citizens can be proud. (See GOVERNMENT; IMMIGRATION; U. S. CONSTITUTION.)

CITRUS FRUITS Oranges, lemons, and all the other fruits in the picture come from plants that are close relatives. They are all citrus fruits. They get the name "citrus" from citron, a fruit more common in Mediterranean lands than in America. Citrus fruits have thick rinds. The pulp inside the fruits is divided into sections.

Kumquat Orange Grapefruit Tangerine Lemon Lime

Oranges are the best-liked of the citrus fruits. Probably they are the best-liked of all fruits. Apples may be more popular in one country and dates in another, but oranges are well liked all over the world. There are many different kinds of oranges. Some kinds are especially good just peeled and eaten as they are. Some are used chiefly for marmalade. Some are best for juice. Navel oranges are among the good eating oranges because they have no seeds. Tangerines, which are a variety of the mandarin orange, are good for eating, too, and they are also very easy to peel.

An orange grove is beautiful. The trees have shiny leaves. The blossoms are white. A tree may have blossoms, green fruit, and ripe golden fruit all at the same time. The flowers are so fragrant that an orange grove can be smelled a long way off.

Grapefruit orchards are beautiful, too. In fact, grapefruit trees would probably be raised for their beauty even if their fruit were not good to eat. The grapefruit got its name because the fruits grow in bunches like bunches of huge grapes.

Lemons and limes are sourer than oranges. We use their juice. Much of it goes into lemonade and limeade.

Kumquats are the smallest of the citrus fruits. They are eaten skin and all.

Citrus fruits are Old World fruits. Their ancestors grew wild in southern Asia. They spread westward to Europe and finally reached America.

Some citrus fruits are man-made. They are crosses between other citrus fruits. The tangelo is a cross between the grapefruit and the tangerine. The citrange is a cross between two different kinds of oranges. The limequat is a cross between the lime and the kumquat.

Citrus fruits not only taste good, but are also good for us. More than 200 years ago a doctor in the British navy found that the juice of lemons and limes would cure sailors who were sick with scurvy. Scurvy was then a common disease. Soon the British navy was providing lemons and limes for all its sailors. So many limes were used that the sailors were called "limeys."

For a long time no one knew why lemons and limes cured scurvy. Now we know that it is because they contain vitamin C. All citrus fruits do. Not only sailors but all of us need vitamin C.

There are miles and miles of citrus groves in the United States. They are all in the South and Southwest, for citrus trees cannot stand cold weather. Frost is the worst enemy of the orchards. Sometimes smudge fires are started in an orchard when there is danger of frost. The smoke makes a blanket that protects the trees.

We can have citrus fruits the year round, for they keep a long time in cold storage. Some of those that are stored are picked before they are fully ripe. They are treated to give them the color of ripe fruit. (See FRUITS; GRAFTING; HYBRIDS.)

The United States is the world's leading producer of oranges.

Coquina Shells (above) and Giant Clam

CLAMS Thousands of animals without backbones have shells. Clams are among them. The shells of clams are always in two parts, or valves. The two valves are held together by a strong hinge.

Clams belong to the big group of animals called mollusks. They are close relatives of the oysters and scallops.

A clam has one foot. This foot is a better tool for burrowing than it is for walking. The foot plows into sand or mud, pulling behind it the sharp edges of the shells. Often all that can be seen of the clam above the sand is the hinge part of the shells.

A pair of tubes called siphons reach from inside the body out beyond the edges of the shells. Water is taken in through one of the siphons. As it goes in, it carries food—tiny plants and animals—and oxygen. The clam has gills that take in the oxygen. The food goes into the digestive system. The water picks up waste products and leaves through the other siphon.

There are many kinds of clams. Some live in fresh water, others in salt water.

Soft-shell clams are found along seashores. They make good chowder. They are sometimes called long-neck clams since they have a neck that may be a foot long.

Pismo Clam

Atlantic Razor Clam

Green Razor Clam

Amethyst Gem Clam

Northern Quahog

Section of Wampum Belt

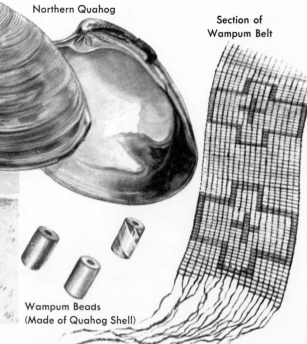

Northern Quahog (With Foot and Siphons Extended)

Wampum Beads
(Made of Quahog Shell)

The neck is made up of the two siphons covered with a leatherlike skin. The siphons point up out of the mud or sand. When the tide is out, little holes and sometimes little spouts of water show where clams are hidden.

Hard-shell clams, or quahogs, are also found along seashores. They, too, are good food. Wampum, Indian money, was made from their shells. Small quahogs are sometimes called littleneck clams.

The giant clam of the Pacific is really a giant. It may weigh 500 pounds, and its shell may be five feet across.

Some fresh-water clams are hitchhikers for a part of their lives. The eggs of these clams hatch inside the mother's body. The little clams stay there for a while. Then they leave through the siphon. Out in the water they die unless they can fasten themselves to the fins or gills of a fish. They travel about on the fish until they grow up. (See MOLLUSKS; OYSTERS; SHELLFISH; SHELLS; STARFISH.)

CLIFF DWELLERS Scattered over the southwestern part of the United States there are many ruined Indian villages like the one in the picture. Some are on the ledges of steep cliffs. Others are in deep caves in the cliffs. Still others are at the foot of cliffs. We call the Indians who built these villages the cliff dwellers.

The villages were built more than 200 years before Columbus discovered America. They had all been given up long before any white men saw them.

The cliff dwellers were farmers. They raised corn and beans on the level land near by. They raised pumpkins and sunflowers, too. They did not have any horses or chickens or pigs or cows. But they did have tame turkeys and dogs.

To add to the food they raised they gathered nuts and berries and killed deer, rabbits, and wild birds. Probably the hunters sometimes brought home bears and porcupines for food.

Cliff dweller villages were well protected.

The women made beautiful baskets and bowls, and they wove cotton cloth. They made jewelry of shells and of turquoise.

Some of the earliest houses were built of sun-dried brick. But the later ones were built of stone fastened together with clay mortar. Many of the walls were covered with plaster. Some of the inside walls had pictures painted on them.

The biggest buildings held many families. Each family, however, had only one room. Some buildings were storage rooms; others were meeting places.

Many houses were built right against the cliff. They had only three walls. The cliff made the back wall. Some rooms were even dug out of the solid rock.

The ruins of the cliff dwellings are all hard to reach. But it is easy to see why the builders chose cliffs as building places. The rock walls protected their villages from wind and rain. More important, they gave protection from enemies.

No one knows the whole story of why the cliff dwellers left their villages. Probably many years of dry weather drove some of them away. We know that, about 650 years ago, there was a period of nearly 30 very dry years. But there may have been other reasons why they left.

Some of the Pueblo Indians of today have customs much like those of the cliff dwellers. Perhaps the Pueblos are their great-great-great-many-times-great-grand-children. (See CAVE MEN.)

Cold winters, . . .

CLIMATE The climate of a place is the year-round weather there. A region may have a dry climate or a wet one. It may have a warm climate or a cold one. The weather may be about the same all through the year, or it may change often. There are many different types of climate.

The climate of a place has a great deal to do with what plants and animals live

warm summers, . . .

there. It also has a great deal to do with how the people of the region live. What they eat and what they wear depend partly on the climate. So do what kinds of houses they build and how they earn a living. Climate even has a great deal to do with how people have fun. (See WEATHER.)

and cool autumns are all part of climate.

CLOCKS AND WATCHES About 1,000 years ago a monk named Gerbert made a timepiece which people called magical. It may have been the first real clock. No one can be sure, for the records do not tell how it worked. But at least there were clocks of a sort in several European monasteries nearly 1,000 years ago.

The first clocks we know much about were made toward the end of the 13th century. Some of them had no hands and no faces. These clocks told time simply by striking the hour. Bells were important parts of early clocks. The word "clock" comes from the French word *cloche,* which means "bell."

The bells of some of the early clocks were struck by hammers held in the hands of little figures of people. These little figures were called "jacks-of-the-clock."

One early clock was three stories tall. Each quarter of the hour was struck by a different jack. The four jacks were figures of a little boy, a middle-aged man, an old man, and a skeleton. At noon there was a procession of twelve little figures, and a cock appeared at the top of the clock, flapped its wings, and crowed. This remarkable clock also told the day of the week, the day of the month, the position of the planets, and the phase of the moon.

Although some of the early clocks were very complicated, none of them were very good timepieces. In all of them a falling weight turned the wheels around. "Winding the clock" in those days meant lifting up the weight to its starting point. Making the wheels turn around was easy. But it was not easy to make the wheels turn at just the right speed. There had to be some way of keeping the weight from falling down in a hurry and sending the wheels spinning around very fast. Ways were worked out of letting the weight move a little way, then stopping it, then letting it move a little more, and so on.

No very good way of making the wheels turn at the right speed was found until the pendulum was invented. The first clocks with pendulums worked much like a grandfather clock of today. In a grandfather clock a weight turns the wheels just as in earlier clocks. As the pendulum in the clock swings back and forth, it moves an arm which does the starting and stopping that make the wheels turn at the right speed. The "ticktock" of a grandfather clock is made as the arm catches one wheel time after time and then lets it go.

When pendulums were put on clocks, minute hands were added, too. There had not been much point in having anything but the hour hands when a clock was likely to gain or lose as much as half an hour in a single day.

About 500 years ago the first watches were made. Of course, there could not be a falling weight in a watch. There could not be a pendulum either. In place of the weight there was a mainspring. In place of the pendulum there was a little flywheel and a very fine spring. Some of the early watches struck the hours, but most did not. The ones that did not strike had to be looked at, or *watched*. It is easy to see how they came to be called watches.

Some of the early watches were called "Nuremberg eggs." They got their name because they were egg-shaped and were made in Nuremberg. They did not tell time very well. None of the early watches did. In fact, they were such poor timekeepers that people called them "ticking toys." Watchmakers were called "toymen."

Soon watchmakers began making beautiful watches. Rich people bought them for their beauty more than for their usefulness. Many people who wore watches carried little pocket sundials to really tell the time.

Watches were made in all sorts of queer shapes: flowers, butterflies, crosses, and even skulls. Some were set in rings. One ring watch, made for a lady, had a little "jack-of-the-clock" that tapped the lady's finger every hour. Many watches had jewels set in their cases.

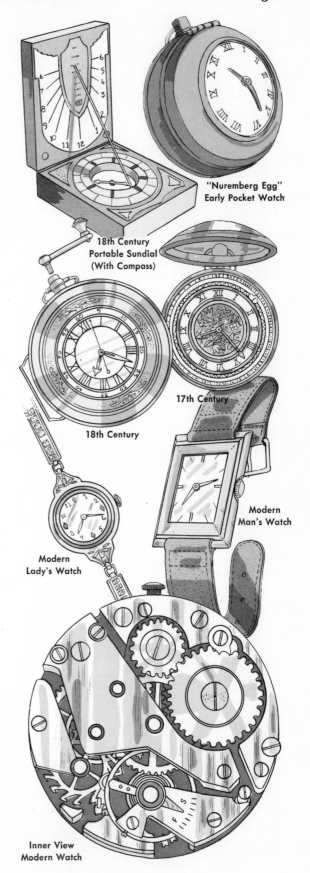

"Nuremberg Egg"
Early Pocket Watch

18th Century
Portable Sundial
(With Compass)

17th Century

18th Century

Modern
Man's Watch

Modern
Lady's Watch

Inner View
Modern Watch

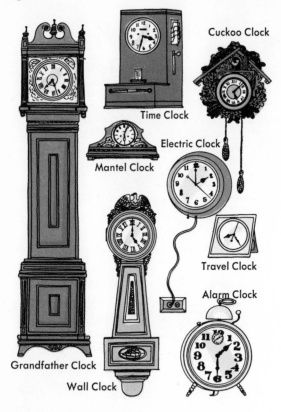

Cuckoo Clock

Time Clock

Electric Clock

Mantel Clock

Travel Clock

Alarm Clock

Grandfather Clock

Wall Clock

HOW A PENDULUM WORKS

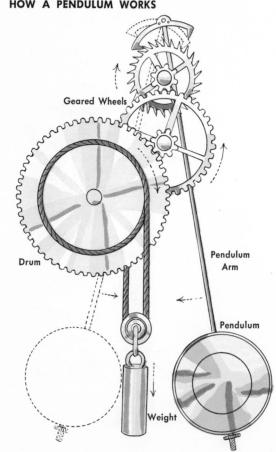

Geared Wheels

Drum

Pendulum Arm

Pendulum

Weight

About 250 years ago watchmakers began using jewels inside watches to make them run better. The rubies and sapphires used are so smooth and hard that they make the friction in the watch much less. The best watches of today have 18 or more jewels, but the jewels are so small that altogether they are worth only a dollar or so.

In 1713 the British government offered a prize of £10,000 to anyone who could make a timepiece that would keep really accurate time. It was 47 years before the prize was won. It was won by a timepiece that lost less than 2 minutes on an ocean voyage of 5 months. The timepiece was called a chronometer. A little later a chronometer was made that lost only 7 seconds on a 46-day voyage. From chronometers, watch and clockmakers found ways of making their clocks and watches better.

Before Americans began to manufacture them, all clocks and watches were handmade. Americans invented machines to do the work. Clocks and watches could be made much more cheaply by machine.

Watches with springs were such a success that clocks began to be made with springs. Clocks could be much smaller if they did not have to have weights and pendulums. Now many clocks have neither springs nor weights. Instead they are run by electricity. Electric clocks are very good and very dependable timekeepers.

When the first watch company of America was founded in 1850, one of the men who worked for this company boasted that his company could make 7 watches a day. His friends laughed. "Where," they asked, "could you sell 7 watches a day?" They did not guess that in less than 100 years watch factories would be making thousands of watches a day and millions of people would be wearing them. (See BELLS; TIME AND TIME TELLING.)

The pull of the weight puts a turning force on the drum and the geared wheels. As the pendulum swings back and forth, its arm lets the wheels turn just so far each time.

CLOTHING OF THE PAST

Egyptian   Greek   Early American and Indian   14th Century European

CLOTHING It would be foolish for an Arab and an Eskimo to dress in the same way. The loose, white robes of the Arab reflect the glaring sunlight and keep him from getting too hot as he goes about in the desert. The Eskimo's two layers of hooded fur suits protect him from the wind and keep him from getting too cold in the icy lands where he lives. Different climates call for different kinds of clothes. For we wear

clothing at least partly for protection from the weather.

We wear clothing for another reason, too—for decoration. Strangely enough, scientists believe that people wore clothing for decoration before they started wearing it for protection. The people of many savage tribes still wear little or no clothing, but they do decorate their bodies. When they want to dress up for a special occasion they may put on feathers, paint, or jewelry.

It used to be easy to tell what country a person was from by looking at his clothes. But clothing habits in many countries are changing. For now that radio and television and airplanes have brought the different parts of the world closer together, ideas about clothes are spreading just as other ideas are. The people of some countries now save the costumes they used to wear every day for holidays. A traveler in Scotland, for instance, might not see any man wearing kilts. Many people in lands like India and China are changing from the kinds of clothing worn in those countries for centuries. Clothes like those worn in the United States are being worn in more and more places. This style of clothing is called "Western dress."

Since clothes are partly for decoration, it is not surprising that styles change. The pictures show a little of the story of how styles have changed. Children's styles have changed over the years just as much as the styles for grownups.

Eskimo

In Colonial America, women made much of the clothing at home.

Some people are not permitted to choose what clothes to wear. They must wear uniforms. A soldier's uniform tells everyone that he is a soldier. It tells, too, something about his duties and what his rank is.

Our earliest ancestors did not have many materials to choose from for their clothing. Animal skins, leaves, and grasses were about the only ones they could use. The first woven fabric that people learned to make was probably linen. They found out how to make linen thousands of years ago.

This cloth is woven from flax fibers. Mummies that have been found in Egyptian tombs were wrapped in linen.

Probably the second cloth that men learned to weave was wool. Wool makes a cloth that is warm and lasts a long time. Cotton and silk, too, go back thousands of years. The people of India were weaving cotton cloth in 2000 B.C. The Chinese carefully guarded the secret of making silk for centuries. Silk was among the riches that traders used to bring back to Europe from the Far East.

Today there are hundreds of materials for clothing, and new ones are being invented. Rayon and nylon are among the rather new fibers used for clothing.

Fortunately, we have given up some styles in clothing that were not good. Women in the United States once had their

CLOTHING OF DIFFERENT TIMES AND PLACES

West Indian
Nobleman of India
Korean
Hopi Indian
Seminole Indian
Scotsman
North Pacific Coast Indian
Greenlander
African
Greek
Peruvian
Hungarian
Tahitian
Burmese
Moslem
Japanese
Chinese
Siberian
17th Century Dutch
American Cowboy
Malayan
Medieval Spaniard
NO SWIMMING
Elizabethan
Dressmaker

dresses made with tiny waists. They had to lace themselves into tight corsets to be able to wear these dresses. Such tight lacing was not good for anyone. Women's dresses, even their everyday dresses, used to sweep the ground. They gathered up much dust and many germs. Children's clothes, especially their dress-up clothes, used to be so "fussy" that the children could not run and play in them.

In most parts of the world people have more clothes than they used to have. Sewing machines help explain why. It is easy to buy ready-made clothes now, too—clothes made in factories. The amount of money the people of the United States spend for ready-made clothes is hard to imagine. It amounts to more than 100 billion dollars a year! (See COTTON; LINEN; NYLON; RAYON; SHOES; WOOL.)

Sudden cloudbursts are frequent in the tropics.

CLOUDBURST   At times rain pours down so fast that it is as if an enormous bag full of water had burst open and spilled all its water at once. A rain of this kind is called a cloudburst.

A cloud cannot really burst. A rain cloud has nothing on the outside to shut in its billions of droplets of water. But, even when the droplets become big drops, strong upward currents of air may keep them from falling. At last, however, the drops are too big and heavy to be held up. They fall with a rush, and we have a cloudburst.

In a cloudburst enough rain to make a layer several inches deep on the ground may fall in a very short time. In Holt, Mo., for instance, 12 inches of rain fell in one hour on June 22, 1947. This is more rain than many parts of the world get in a year. And in Jefferson, Iowa, two-thirds of an inch fell in just one minute on July 10, 1955! (See FLOODS; RAIN; U.S. WEATHER BUREAU; WEATHER.)

CLOUDS   On some days no blue sky shows. The sky is covered all over with a layer of clouds. On other days the clouds do not cover the whole sky, but big white clouds go sailing by. Sometimes there are feathery clouds high in the sky. Sometimes, too, there are dark storm clouds.

Clouds are made mostly of tiny drops of water or of tiny crystals of ice. They are like the little clouds over the whistle of a steam engine, or like those from a person's breath on a winter day.

Storm clouds may be dark because a great deal of dust has been blown up into them. But usually clouds are dark simply because they are too thick to let much sunlight through. Even if clouds are dark from below, they are glistening white on top.

The big, fluffy white clouds towering high into the air are cumulus clouds. Their tops are sometimes several miles above the ground. "Cumulus" means "pile."

The clouds that make a gray layer over the whole sky are called stratus clouds. "Stratus" means "layer."

The feathery white clouds are cirrus clouds. "Cirrus" means "curl." These clouds sometimes look like curls of smoke. Some cirrus clouds are so long and narrow that they are called "mare's tails." Cirrus clouds are high above the ground—usually at least seven or eight miles high.

Some clouds are part cirrus, part cumulus. Clouds of this kind make a "mackerel sky." There are many other "in-between" clouds, too. Often two or three kinds of clouds can be seen at the same time.

The drops of water or bits of ice in clouds are usually very tiny. They are so tiny that more than 100 million of them could be put in the bowl of a teaspoon. At the center of each drop of water or crystal of ice there is usually an even tinier speck of dust. The water and ice in clouds come from the water vapor in the air. The water vapor is more likely to change to drops of water or

Cumulus Clouds

Stratus Clouds

Cirrus Clouds

Mackerel Sky

crystals of ice if there is a solid speck of something in the air for the water or ice to form around.

Clouds travel. The wind blows them about. Sometimes clouds move across the sky as fast as an airplane.

The sky may be very cloudy at one moment. Rain or snow may be falling from the clouds. But half an hour later the clouds may have disappeared, and the sun may be shining brightly.

Clouds sometimes disappear because the wind blows them out of sight. They sometimes disappear because the water or ice in them evaporates. The water or ice changes back, that is, into invisible water vapor. A cloud may disappear because the water or ice in it has fallen to the ground as rain or snow. A dark cloud may not disappear after rain or snow has fallen from it. But it is almost sure to be lighter.

Many people have gone right through clouds in airplanes. Going through a cloud is like going through a heavy fog. No wonder! A fog is a cloud close to the ground. (See FOG; RAIN; U. S. WEATHER BUREAU; WATER; WEATHER.)

CLUB MOSSES Names do not always tell a true story. Ground pine, the little plant shown in the circle in the picture, is not a kind of pine. Instead it is a club moss. Club mosses, in turn, are not really mosses. They are, instead, much closer relatives of the ferns.

There are several hundred kinds of club mosses. Some, like the different kinds of ground pine, grow in northern forests. But many live only in very warm lands.

Club mosses have small leaves. The leaves grow close to the stems.

These plants never bloom. They do not produce seeds. New plants grow from tiny balls of living material called spores. Many simple plants grow from spores.

All the club mosses of today are little plants. But 250 million years ago, during the Coal Age, the story was very different. Then giant club mosses were among the tallest trees in the forests. And there were enormous numbers of them. Much of our coal was made from the forests in which these giant club mosses grew.

There were still giant club mosses in the early days of the dinosaurs. But the club mosses could not hold their own with the seed plants, which by that time had begun to "take the earth." Only small kinds of club mosses were able to live on. But whenever we come across ground pine in the woods or see it used in Christmas decorations, it will perhaps remind us that its ancestors were once among the world's leading plants. (See COAL; FERNS; HORSETAILS; PLANT KINGDOM.)

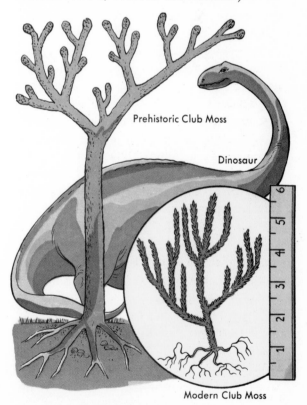

Prehistoric Club Moss

Dinosaur

Modern Club Moss

Life in the Coal Age

COAL Marco Polo had many wonderful stories to tell when he came home to Venice from China more than 600 years ago. One of his stories was that the Chinese used a kind of black rock as fuel. Not many people believed him. Whoever heard of burning rock? But now so much of this black rock is burned that it keeps thousands of people busy digging it out of the ground. The black rock, of course, is coal.

Coal is sometimes called "black diamond." It gets this name because it is mostly carbon and diamonds are crystals of carbon. Another nickname for coal is "buried sunshine." It gets this name because it was made from forests of long ago. To grow, the forests had to have sunshine.

The story of some of our coal begins 300 million years ago in a time that is called the Coal Age. Much of the world then was warm. And much of the land was swampy. Great forests grew in the swamps. They did not look like our forests now. The trees were mostly giant ferns and giant club mosses and giant horsetails.

In the forests no birds flew in and out among the trees. There were no birds in those days. But there were dragonflies and cockroaches bigger than any we have now. There were no lizards or squirrels. In fact, there were few reptiles and no furry animals at all. But there were giant amphibians, ancient relatives of the toads and frogs of today.

None of the trees in the forests were ever cut down. The time was long before the time of the first people. But trees died and fell over into the shallow water, and other trees grew in their places. The dead trees did not all rot away. Something in the water kept them from doing so. The bottom of the swamps came to be covered with a thick layer of half-rotted plant material. It was much like the peat found in peat bogs today.

After a long, long time the water in the swamps became so deep that the forests were drowned. Perhaps the land sank. Perhaps the oceans rose and flooded the land. No one knows which. The drowned trees fell over and made the layer of plant material at the bottom of the water thicker. Mud washed in on top of it.

The same thing happened not once but many times. The land rose or the oceans sank, and the land was swampy again. Forests grew. The land sank or the oceans rose, and the forests were drowned and covered with mud. There came to be layers at the bottom of the water like the layers in a layer cake. The layers of "cake" were the layers of half-rotted plants. The mud was the "frosting" between the layers.

Finally the great swamps became dry land. The layers of half-rotted plants had been squeezed into thinner layers of black material. It hardened into coal. The mud hardened into the rock we call shale.

The Coal Age ended about 200 million years ago. But some coal was made later.

All coal was made from plants. But there are different kinds of coal. Ordinary black coal is often called soft coal. An-

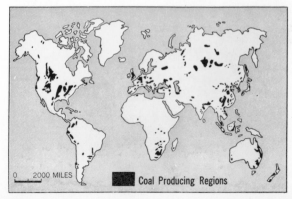

Coal Producing Regions

other name for it is bituminous coal. Some coal, after it was made, was squeezed so much that it became much harder than ordinary coal. It is called hard coal, or "anthracite." "As black as coal" is a common saying, but not all coal is black. Lignite is brown instead. Lignite is softer than soft coal. It was not made so long ago. Cannel coal is black, but it lights much more easily than common coal. The name "cannel" comes from "candle."

Peat is sometimes called "unfinished coal." If peat were buried under layers of mud for thousands of years, it would finally turn into coal.

Some layers of coal are so near the surface that we can get the coal just by shoveling off the rock and soil on top. Mining of this kind, usually done with giant power shovels, is called strip mining.

Much coal mining is shaft mining. A big hole, or shaft, is dug down into a layer of coal. Then the miners work out in all directions from the bottom of the shaft.

Working in a deep coal mine used to be very dangerous. Now many things have been done to make the danger less. Mines, for instance, are now ventilated. And miners no longer wear lamps that are likely to set fire to gases and cause explosions.

Oil and natural gas have taken the place of coal somewhat. But for some uses nothing can take its place. So far as anyone can see, we shall keep on needing millions of tons of this black rock every year. (See EARTH HISTORY; FUELS; PEAT.)

Mining used to be done with a pick and shovel.

ANTHRACITE

BITUMINOUS

LIGNITE

Elevator

Gallery

Turntable from Main Shaft

Pit Pony

Mining by Drilling

Opening New Gallery

Mining by Saw and Moving Belt

Various mine scenes are combined in this picture.

COAL TAR

Dye

Perfume

Flavoring

Paint

Insect Killer

Film

Plastics

Medicine

Saccharine

Freon

Explosives

Weed Killer

COAL TAR Much of the coal we mine is used in making coke. When coke is made from coal, a sticky black liquid called coal tar is left over. Coal tar used to be thrown away. But now so many uses have been found for it that it is as valuable as the coal itself. It makes a good fuel. Besides, hundreds of products are manufactured from it. The chart shows some of them. Who would guess that such things as perfumes and dyes and flavorings could come from something that was once just a nuisance?

The first step in getting the products from coal tar is to heat the tar in big closed tanks. Pipes lead off from the tanks. Coal tar is a mixture of many chemicals. As it is heated, first one chemical and then another is driven off through the pipes. The many products of coal tar are made from these chemicals. (See COAL; DYES; FLAVORINGS; PERFUME.)

COCONUT A cluster of coconut palms is a common sight on the shores of warm seas. The seeds of these palms are called coconuts. Coconuts are among the biggest seeds in the world.

A coconut has a thick husk around it when it comes from the tree. Fibers from this husk can be used in making coarse cloth and rope. They can also be used in weaving such things as hats and baskets and mats.

But the seed inside the husk is much more important. The seed has thick walls of white "meat." The coconut we eat in candy, cakes, and pies is made by cutting this meat into shreds. The meat has much oil in it. Some of the meat, instead of being eaten, is used to furnish coconut oil. This oil may be used for cooking. Much of it finds its way into margarine, soap, and face cream. The center of the coconut is filled with a clear liquid called coconut milk or coconut water. It is good to drink fresh from the coconut. Many recipes for cooking other foods call for coconut milk.

It is not easy for anyone except a monkey to gather coconuts from coconut palms. These palms may be as tall as a ten-story building. And there are no branches to catch hold of.

Even if they did not bear coconuts, coconut palms would be worth having. Their huge leaves are useful in making thatched roofs for homes. Their trunks can be used in building. In fact, every part of the coconut palm has some value. (See SEEDS.)

The gently swaying coconut palm is a common sight in tropical regions around the world.

Both green and ripe coconuts are available all the year round.

COFFEE Many men and women think that a day cannot start right without coffee for breakfast. Coffee is probably the best liked of all hot drinks. Americans drink more than 140 billion cups of coffee in a year's time.

Coffee is made from coffee beans. Coffee beans are not really beans. But they are seeds just as beans are. They are formed in red berries. Each berry has two seeds in it. The plant on which the berries grow is a bush from five to fifteen feet tall.

Coffee grows only in warm lands. It cannot stand the least bit of frost. But it cannot stand great heat, either. Many coffee plantations are on mountain slopes, where the air is cooler than in the lowlands. Coffee needs rich soil. It needs much rain while the berries are forming and much sunshine while the berries are ripening. Most of our coffee comes to us from northern South America and from the countries of Central America.

A coffee plantation is a beautiful sight when the coffee bushes are in bloom. The blossoms show very white against the glossy green leaves. They are as fragrant as orange blossoms. When the flowers drop their petals the berries appear. At first they are tiny and green. As they get larger they change first to yellow, then to bright red. When they are ripe they are dark red. Some may be almost black.

The berries are picked when they are ripe. The next step is to take all the outer part of the berry away from the beans inside. There are two ways of doing so—the "dry" way and the "wet" way.

In the dry way the berries are washed quickly. Then they are spread out in the sun and left there for three or four weeks. They are raked or stirred often so that they will dry evenly. When the berries are dry and shriveled, the beans are hulled. After several more days of drying they are ready to be shipped.

The wet way is a faster way. The outside covering of the berry is taken off at once. Then the pulp is made to ferment. It gets so soft that it can be washed off the seeds. The seeds are then dried.

Before coffee beans are used, they must be roasted and ground. Coffee does not keep its flavor long after it is roasted. The beans that are to be shipped to another country are therefore shipped "green," which means "before roasting."

Not all coffee has the same flavor. Coffee in the stores is, as a rule, a mixture of two or more kinds. Mixing coffee of different kinds is called blending. Most people who like coffee very much have a favorite blend.

Drinking coffee in the evening may keep a person awake. There is an old Arab story that tells how some shepherds were kept awake at night by their animals. The animals were romping about instead of sleeping. The shepherds found that the animals were eating the berries from some wild bushes. They decided to eat some of the berries themselves. They did, and they felt very energetic. In this way, the story says, people first found out about coffee. (See BRAZIL; CENTRAL AMERICA; SOUTH AMERICA.)

Young coffee berries are green. As they ripen, they turn a rich red. Inside each berry are two beans which are roasted.

After roasting they take on the familiar brown color of coffee.

Workers turn coffee beans drying in the sun.

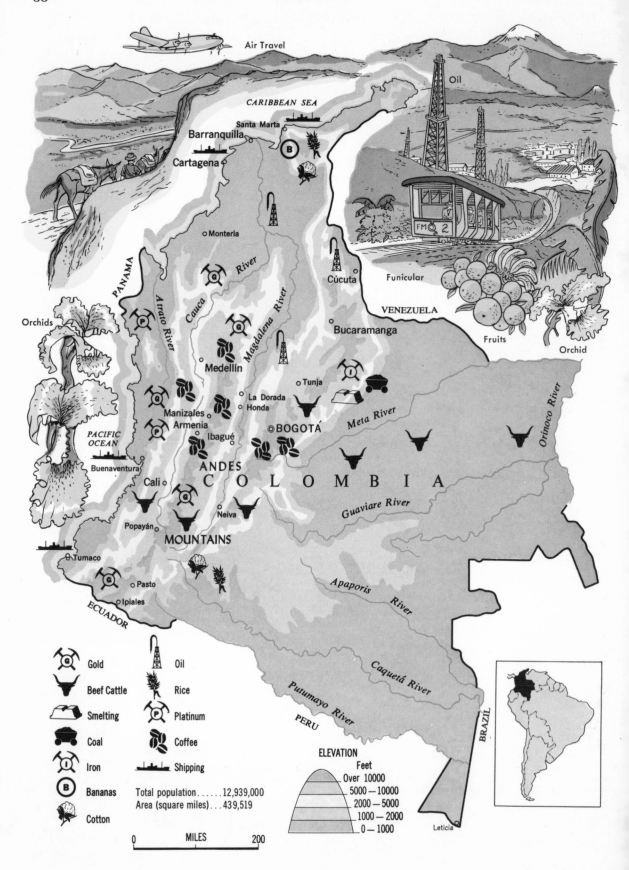

Air Travel

CARIBBEAN SEA

Oil

Santa Marta

Barranquilla

Cartagena

B

Funicular

VENEZUELA

Orchids

PANAMA

Atrato River

Cauca River

Montería

Cúcuta

Magdalena River

Bucaramanga

Medellín

Manizales

Armenia

La Dorada

Honda

Tunja

Meta River

BOGOTÁ

Ibagué

PACIFIC OCEAN

Buenaventura

Cali

ANDES

C O L O M B I A

Guaviare River

Neiva

Popayán

MOUNTAINS

Orinoco River

Tumaco

G

Pasto

Ipiales

ECUADOR

Apaporis River

Putumayo River

Caquetá River

PERU

Fruits

Orchid

Oil

Rice

Platinum

Coffee

Shipping

Gold

Beef Cattle

Smelting

Coal

Iron

Bananas

Cotton

B

Total population......12,939,000
Area (square miles)...439,519

ELEVATION
Feet
Over 10000
5000 — 10000
2000 — 5000
1000 — 2000
0 — 1000

Leticia

BRAZIL

0   MILES   200

COLOMBIA Only one country in South America has seacoasts on both the Pacific Ocean and the Caribbean Sea. This country is Colombia.

The country was named Colombia for Christopher Columbus. But for many years before it was given that name, Spanish settlers there called it New Granada.

Colombia is a land of very high mountains, high plateau land, and much hot, wet lowland. Some of that lowland is along the Pacific. Some is along the Caribbean. The whole southeastern part of Colombia is lowland, too. Between it and the other lowlands there are mountains.

The mountains are the Andes. Some of the peaks are so high that they are snowcapped all year around, even though they are near the equator. The plateau land and mountain valleys are pleasantly cool.

The southeastern lowland is much shut off from the rest of the world. The few people who live there are mostly Indians.

Some of the people of Colombia are pure Spanish. Some are Negroes. They are descendants of slaves brought to the new land by the Spaniards. Most of the other people are part Indian and part Spanish.

There are some cities along the coasts. But far more than half of all the Colombians live in the highlands.

Bogotá, the capital, is a pleasant, highland city of more than a million people. Spaniards settled there long ago. But Bogotá was hard to reach. For many years few newcomers came to it. Even as late as 25 years ago, the journey to it from the Caribbean coast took from 4 to 20 days. It was first by train, then by river boat, then by train, then by boat again, and then by train. On the last part of the trip, the train climbed more than 7,000 feet.

Airlines now make travel to Bogotá easy. But much that early Spaniards brought there still remains. The language is Spanish. So are many of the customs.

The first airline in the Western Hemisphere was Colombian. Today, Colombian airlines are famous for the many tons of cargo they carry. Little planes called "air taxis" carry some of it. They fly even to a few places in the southeastern lowland, and to some small high places.

The chief crop of Colombia is coffee. It is raised on slopes in the lower parts of the highlands. Wheat, oats, barley, and potatoes grow on higher land. On the lowland near the Caribbean, sugar, rice, tobacco, cotton, and bananas are raised.

Colombia is rich in oil and minerals. Oil is piped to the Caribbean coast. There are mines in the Andes and along the Pacific. The world's most famous emerald mines are in Colombia. Other mines there produce silver, gold, and platinum.

The country has stores of unmined minerals. It has great forests that are not yet being cut, and much grazing land. Improved ways of work are being found. No wonder Colombia sometimes is called a "land of the future." (See ANDES; BOLÍVAR, SIMÓN; SOUTH AMERICA.)

Jaguar

Flag

Tequendama Falls

Sugar Cane Shoots

Fruit Vendor

Church of Veracruz

Stone Idol

COLONIAL LIFE IN AMERICA Axes ringing in the forests, great trees falling, log cabins rising like magic—these were early colonial days in America. In the cabins mothers prepared food in open fireplaces in black iron kettles. Families ate their meals on homemade wooden tables. They sat on stools. Their mugs were of English pewter and their plates of American "dishwood." There was one bed—for father and mother—fastened into the logs of a corner. Children slept on sacks of dried leaves covered with furs. A few families had brought a little furniture from England.

The mother made the clothes for the family. She spun linen and woolen yarns on the spinning wheel. The children helped her dye these yarns with goldenrod and berry juices. She wove the yarns into cloth, usually called homespun, on a hand loom. From deer skins she made clothes for father and the boys.

Outside the cabin lay the cornfield among tree stumps. Near by was the garden of pumpkins and beans.

With time, life in the New England colonies, the middle colonies, and the South came to be rather different. Later settlers from England and other European countries brought their own customs with them. The soil, climate, and building materials in the three sections were not the same. They helped to bring about differences in ways of living.

In New England most people lived in small towns with their farms outside the town. These settlements were near the sea or tucked snugly into mountain valleys. Cabins slowly disappeared as houses of frame or stone were built. The roofs of the houses sloped steeply to shed the heavy snows. Women still cooked in open fireplaces of stone. Men went out to their farms by day. The tall steeple of the white frame church looked down on each town.

Mother now did not make all the clothes. The town dressmaker and the shoemaker came to work in many homes for several days each year. Some people could afford to buy cloth from England. They bought furniture, too, and table silver.

In towns there were enough people to support a public school. Families paid for their children's schooling in money or farm products or fish. They took turns furnishing firewood to the school. If they furnished no wood, their children had to sit far from the fire. Classroom work in school was based on the "three R's"—reading, writing, and arithmetic.

New England children had many chores. Boys helped to collect stones from the rocky fields and to build them into stone fences. Boys and girls picked sackfuls of bayberries for their mothers' candlemaking. In seaport towns boys helped with shipbuilding. Many got their "sea legs" early and later became ship captains.

New Englanders were very strict about attending church. Services lasted all day.

Dutch homes and canals made colonial Manhattan look like Holland.

People carried their dinners and ate them between services in the church or the churchyard. During the long sermons the tithing-man kept the children awake. He had a long pole with a brass knob on one end and a squirrel's tail on the other.

In the middle colonies there were Dutch, German, Scotch, Irish, and English settlements. Many of the English settlers were Quakers. Farms, big and little, spread over broad valleys. The winters were more mild than in New England. Wheat and corn grew well. The farmers had flour and cornmeal and cattle to sell to the people of the towns. Children went to church schools.

The Dutch settlers on the island of Manhattan, where New York City now stands, wanted their island to be like their beloved Holland. They made the marshy rivers look like the canals of Holland. Their tall, narrow, brick houses faced the "canals." Windmills ground their grain. In winter children had fun skating. Girls wore full red skirts. The boys wore long, baggy breeches, red stockings, and beaver caps.

The Dutch homes in America were much like those of Holland. The beds were built into the walls like cupboards. There were leather chairs from Holland. The fireplace was decorated with blue-and-white tiles. Housewives scrubbed their floors often and covered them with sand. Father and the boys ate dinner with their hats on.

The southern colonies had few towns. The farmers lived on their farms, separated by forests. A few of these settlers had large plantations. The planter's great house was

Tobacco was shipped in big barrels from the private wharves of the Southern plantations.

All the children had to help with the work in colonial days.

built of brick. His green lawn, with shade trees and flower gardens, sloped down to a broad river. Near the great house were smaller buildings—the family school-house, the kitchen, and the dairy, stables, carriage house, and workshops. Farther away were the log cabins of the Negro slaves. Most of the slaves worked in the tobacco or rice fields during the long, hot summers. Some were house servants. Some worked in the shops making tobacco barrels and shoes, and spinning and weaving for the plantation.

The rivers were the chief highways in the South. Ships from England came up the rivers to the planter's private dock. They brought fine clothes, silver, china, and books. These ships carried away rice and tobacco for English buyers. Sometimes they brought a private teacher for the planter's children. Sometimes they carried the planter's older sons to school in England. The plantations were so widely scattered that it was not easy to have public schools. The dancing master and the music teacher came to give lessons at the great house. Guests often came from distant plantations to parties and dances.

Colonial children liked many of the same games that children play today. They liked to play ball and bat, shuffleboard, and tag, to shoot marbles, and to bowl on the grass. In spring and autumn they liked to go with their fathers and mothers to town or country fairs. There they saw the farmers exhibiting their fruits and vegetables, and their finest horses, cattle, and hogs. They watched horse racing, puppet shows, and ropewalking. One thing they disliked—and no wonder—was taking big spoonfuls of medicine made of wine mixed with herbs, earthworms, and sometimes even with powdered toads. (See MAYFLOWER; NEW ENGLAND; PILGRIMS; SMITH, JOHN; THANKSGIVING.)

The coming of a ship was a big event.

COLOR No one could see the rose at the top of the page if there weren't any light shining on the picture. Light has to shine on the picture and then bounce up to our eyes. Then why are the petals red and the sepals green? Since it is just sunlight or artificial light that reaches our eyes, why isn't everything the same color?

To understand color one has to know that sunlight is made of many colors. A rainbow shows the colors in sunlight. Tiny drops of water in the air cause a rainbow by breaking up sunlight into the colors it is made of. Most artificial light is very much like sunlight.

When sunlight falls on the picture of the rose, the flower does not reflect all the sunlight. The ink used for the petals soaks up, or absorbs, most of the colors in the sunlight that strikes it. But it does not soak up the red rays. It reflects them to our eyes. The petals look red because the red rays reach our eyes.

The sepals soak up the red rays. But they do not absorb the green rays. They reflect them to our eyes. The sepals therefore look green. The color of anything depends on the rays of light that it sends back to our eyes.

White is a mixture of all the colors in the rainbow. The paper of this page looks white because it sends back to our eyes all the colors in the light that reaches it. Black is no color at all. The letters on this page are black because the black ink absorbs all the colors that strike it. The letters would not show if the paper around them did not reflect light to our eyes.

There are special lamps that do not give off white light like sunlight. A mercury vapor lamp, for instance, gives off light with no red rays in it. A person looks very unhealthy in the light of a mercury vapor lamp. His lips are purple and his cheeks bluish because no red rays are reaching them to be reflected. Some lamps send out only red rays. In the light of such a lamp the petals of the rose would still look red. But the sepals could not look green. No green light reaches them to be reflected. The sepals would therefore look black.

There is an easy way of showing that white light is made up of all the colors of the rainbow. If a disk made up of the rainbow colors is whirled around very fast, the separate colors do not show. The eye puts them all together. The disk looks white.

Another easy way to see that white light is made up of all the colors of the rainbow is to look through a prism. The prism acts like the tiny drops of water that cause rainbows. Everything you see through a prism looks as if it has a rainbow border. (See LIGHT; RAINBOW.)

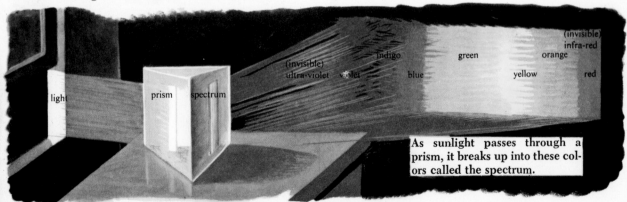

As sunlight passes through a prism, it breaks up into these colors called the spectrum.

COLORADO The state of Colorado was named for a mighty river which is bordered by reddish stone cliffs. Long ago, Spanish explorers named that river the Colorado. The name means "reddish."

Only seven states are larger than Colorado. This big, very wide state straddles the widest part of the great Rocky Mountains. Very high ranges in the Rockies run north and south in central Colorado. The western part of the state is a rough, dry plateau. Eastern Colorado is in the Great Plains. It, too, gets little rain.

The Rockies in Colorado form part of the Great Divide between rivers that flow to the Atlantic and those that flow to the Pacific. Among the Atlantic rivers that rise in Colorado are the South Platte, the Arkansas, and the Rio Grande. The Colorado is a Pacific river.

Only 11 states are newer than Colorado. It became a state in 1876, a hundred years after the Declaration of Independence. For a good reason, then, one of Colorado's nicknames is Centennial State.

The United States bought part of the land of Colorado from France, in the Louisiana Purchase of 1803, and part of it from Spain in 1848. But American pioneers were in no hurry to settle in that land until after men found gold in it late in the 1850's. Then many settlers came in the "Race for the Rockies" and the Pikes Peak gold rush. By 1860, Denver, now Colorado's "mile-high" capital, was a small city. It grew even more after a railroad from the East reached the city in 1870.

Another nickname for Colorado is Silver State. Colorado's mines now produce silver, gold, lead, coal, uranium, molybdenum, and other minerals. The state is well-known for its great mineral wealth.

In spite of its light rainfall, Colorado is chiefly a farming state. It has cattle ranches and dairy farms. It also has farms on which grains, vegetables, sugar beets, and fruits are raised. Colorado potatoes and Rocky Ford melons are famous. So are the cherries, apples, and peaches from the orchards of mountain farmers. Irrigation in many places makes big crops possible. California is the only state which has more irrigated land than Colorado.

Factories and mills employ many people. Denver is a great meat-packing center. Much mining machinery is made there, too. From tons of sugar beets, refiners make sugar. Pueblo has big steel mills.

Each year thousands of visitors spend vacations in Colorado. Rocky Mountain National Park has been called America's favorite playground. In Mesa Verde National Park, the prehistoric homes of cliff dwellers can be seen. And there are many scattered wonders, such as great dunes, deep gorges, and Pikes Peak. That peak is one of 54 Colorado peaks more than 14,000 feet high. Excellent places to fish attract many visitors. And airlines link Denver to places near and far. (See CLIFF DWELLERS.)

Fishing	Skiing	Horseback Riding

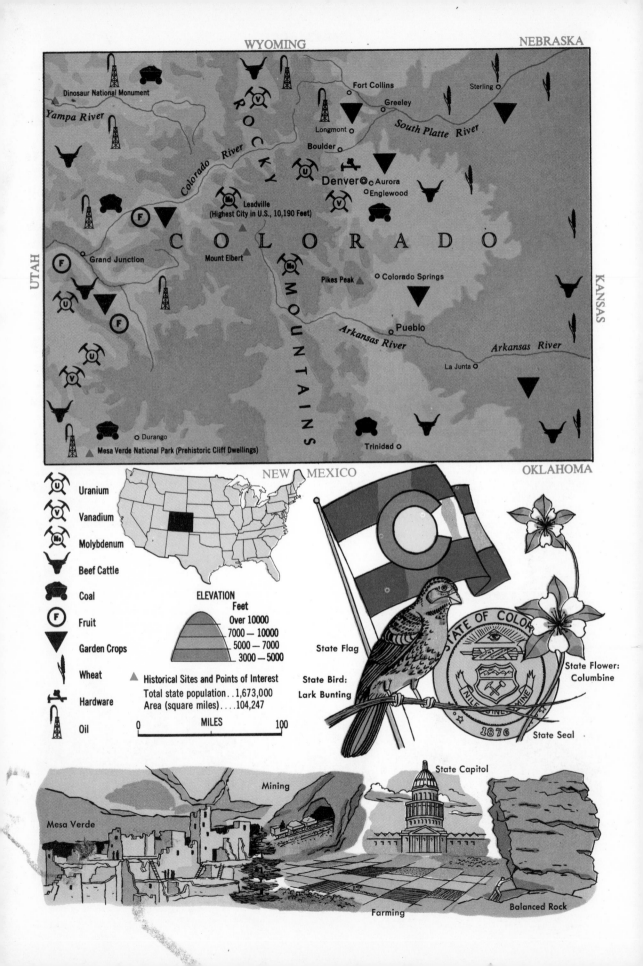

WYOMING   NEBRASKA

Dinosaur National Monument

Yampa River

R
O
C
K
Y

Fort Collins

Sterling

Greeley

South Platte River

Longmont

Boulder

Colorado River

Denver

Aurora

Englewood

Leadville
(Highest City in U.S., 10,190 Feet)

C O L O R A D O

Grand Junction

Mount Elbert

Pikes Peak

Colorado Springs

M
O
U
N
T
A
I
N
S

Pueblo

Arkansas River

Arkansas River

La Junta

Durango

Mesa Verde National Park (Prehistoric Cliff Dwellings)

Trinidad

UTAH

KANSAS

NEW MEXICO   OKLAHOMA

Uranium

Vanadium

Molybdenum

Beef Cattle

Coal

Fruit

Garden Crops

Wheat

Hardware

Oil

ELEVATION
Feet
Over 10000
7000 — 10000
5000 — 7000
3000 — 5000

▲ Historical Sites and Points of Interest

Total state population . . 1,673,000

Area (square miles) 104,247

0   MILES   100

State Flag

State Bird:
Lark Bunting

State Flower:
Columbine

STATE OF COLOR
1876
State Seal

Mesa Verde

Mining

State Capitol

Farming

Balanced Rock

COLUMBUS, CHRISTOPHER (1446-1506) It was Friday, the 3rd of August, 1492. Three small ships set sail from Palos in Spain. They were the "Santa María," the "Pinta," and the "Niña." Fewer than 100 men were on board them. The ships were on their way over an unmapped sea to find a new route to the Far East. Their commander was Christopher Columbus.

Columbus was born in Genoa, Italy, a city of seafarers. By the time he was 30 he had gone to sea many times. On one voyage he had sailed as far as Iceland.

In those days every nation in Europe wanted to find a short trade route to the Far East. Spices and gold and silk had to be carried over long land routes from Asia to Europe. Perhaps a shorter and easier route by sea could be found.

No one knows exactly when Columbus first had the idea of sailing west to find the Far East. But at least by the time he was 30 he was eager to try out this idea. Along with many people of his time, Columbus was sure that the earth is round. Since the earth is round, he thought, and since Asia stretches so very far eastward, it must curve a large part of the way around the earth. China and India, he argued, could

not be very far to the west. He did not guess how big the earth is.

Columbus first asked the King of Portugal for men and ships. The King said no. He favored finding a way around Africa.

Then Columbus went to King Ferdinand and Queen Isabella of Spain. They were interested, but they thought that Columbus wanted too much reward if he was successful. He wanted a tenth of all the riches he brought back. He also wanted to be made "Admiral of the Ocean Sea." At first they, too, said no. But as Columbus was on his way to ask help from the King of France, they changed their minds and gave him the ships he wanted.

After leaving Palos, the little ships sailed to the Canary Islands. From there, on September 9, they headed due west into unknown waters. The winds blew steadily and pushed them on their way.

For weeks the ships sailed westward. The crew grew restless. Never before had they been out of sight of land for so long.

As time went by with no land appearing, the men threatened to mutiny. Columbus is said to have urged them on by crying "Adelante! Adelante!" ("Sail on! Sail on!")

Columbus kept a journal on the voyage. For October 10 it reads, "Here the people could endure no longer." But once again

Columbus convinced Ferdinand and Isabella that he could find a shorter route to the East.

The weary weeks dragged on for the men in their tiny ships.

he persuaded the men to sail on. Two nights later they sighted land. At daybreak they landed. Columbus named the island where they landed San Salvador. It is in the group now called the Bahamas.

Columbus sailed from island to island. His men were disappointed that they found no great, rich cities. There were only a few villages. Dark-skinned people lived in them. Since Columbus thought he was close to India, he called the natives Indians. After two or three months of sailing among the islands, Columbus returned to Spain.

The rulers of Spain were excited. In a short time Columbus was on his way back with 17 ships and over 1,000 men. But again he found only islands.

On Columbus' third voyage to the New World, he reached the coast of South America. But he thought it was just another island in his way to the Far East. This time he was taken back to Spain in chains.

Back in Spain he was soon forgiven. He even made another trip to the New World. But still he found no riches. He died believing that America was only a group of islands on the way to the Far East.

We know now that Columbus and his men were not the first white men to reach America. Norsemen had sailed to North America a long time before Columbus. But other people did not find out about the journeys of the Norsemen till many centuries later. Almost all Europe knew about the voyages of Columbus soon after they were over. He became famous for discovering America. (See AMERICAS; EXPLORERS; HISTORY; LEIF THE LUCKY; VIKINGS; WEST INDIES.)

COLUMBUS' SHIPS

A comet's tail is formed as it nears the sun.

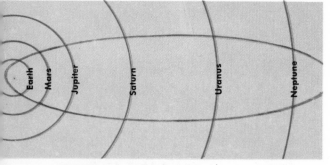

The very long orbit of Halley's comet cuts through the paths of several planets.

COMET The sun has a whole family of heavenly bodies traveling around it. Some of the most interesting are the comets. "Comet" comes from a Latin word that means "hair." A comet looks like a star that has shining hair streaming out from it.

There are hundreds of comets in our solar system, but many people have never seen one. Most comets do not come close enough to the earth to be seen without a telescope.

People of long ago were very much frightened when there was a comet bright enough to be seen. They thought it was a sign that something terrible was about to happen. Today people have given up that old idea.

Comets have paths around the sun just as the earth has. But their paths differ in shape. They are like a long oval. The paths of many comets cross the earth's path. Some day the earth may have a head-on collision with a comet. It has already gone through the tail of one. This happened on

Halley's comet, expected about every 76 years, last appeared in 1910

May 18, 1910. Newspapers carried the news in advance. Many people feared the world would end. But nothing happened at all. If the news had not been in the papers, few people would have known that the earth had had a strange adventure.

No one knows what would happen if the earth ran into the head of a comet. The head of a comet is very big—much larger than the earth—but it is not a solid ball. Scientists believe it is made up of millions of chunks of rock and iron surrounded by gas. Possibly the earth would be badly damaged if it did hit the head of a comet.

When a comet is far away from the sun, it does not have a tail. But when a comet comes close to the sun, the light of the sun drives out some of the gas in the head. This forms a tail which shines in the sunlight. A comet's tail always streams out away from the sun.

Halley's comet is the most famous comet. It was named for Edmund Halley, a famous English astronomer. Halley's comet comes

close to the earth every 76 years. It was through the tail of this comet that the earth passed in 1910. This same comet was seen during the Crusades when the Christians were fighting the Turks. One of the Christians' prayers was "Lord, save us from the Devil, the Turk, and the Comet."

Sometimes a comet goes too close to the sun or a large planet and is pulled to pieces. Nothing is left of it but bits of rock and iron. All the comets may finally be destroyed. (See ASTRONOMY; METEORS AND METEORITES; SOLAR SYSTEM.)

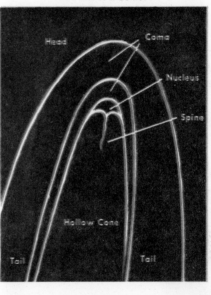

The Parts of a Comet

The nucleus, or center, of a comet may be as large as the earth. The head, or coma, surrounds the nucleus and is far larger. The tail, which streams behind the comet, is sometimes as long as the distance from the earth to the sun.

1910
Halley's Comet

1861
Great Comet

1908
Morehouse's Comet

A Communist Youth Group

COMMUNICATION

A person often wishes to share an idea with someone else. People always are eager to get news of interesting happenings. Passing along ideas and news is called communication.

Making gestures and talking were probably the first ways of communicating. Later men learned to draw pictures, to write, and much later, to print. They learned to send signals with drums and smoke and mirrors. They worked out ways for messengers to travel fast from place to place.

During the past 100 years many new ways of communicating have been invented. Today we have the telegraph, the telephone, and the radio. We have message cables which cross oceans. We have moving pictures and filmstrips. Our newest means of communication is television. (See CABLES, SUBMARINE; RADIO; TELEGRAPH; TELEPHONE; TELEVISION.)

Sending a Message by Smoke Signals

COMMUNISM

In the United States many people own their own homes, farms, and businesses. Everyone is free to choose the kind of work he wants to do. In communist countries, things are quite different. Under communism, the state owns all the land and runs all the businesses. The goal is for no one to be rich and no one poor. All are supposed to work and share equally.

The term "communism" has been used for only a little more than 100 years. It came into use after *The Communist Manifesto* was written by Karl Marx and Friedrich Engels of Germany. The first country to be ruled by a communist government is the Soviet Union. Under the leadership of Nikolai Lenin and others, communists took control of the country by force in the Bolshevik (BOL she vik) Revolution of 1917.

To some people, communism sounds like a pleasant way of living. The Soviet Union and Communist China have certainly made great advances in science and industry. But life has not been very pleasant in any country where communism has been tried. Communist rulers have enforced their rule harshly. The people have had very little freedom. They have been told not only what work they must do, but also what they should think, study, and believe.

People who believe in communism are often called "reds," because red is the main color in the communist flag. Because of the lack of freedom in communist countries "communist" and "red" are dreaded words to many. (See SOCIALISM; UNION OF SOVIET SOCIALIST REPUBLICS.)

The Romans sailed without compasses.

COMPASS, MAGNETIC For hundreds of years after men had boats they still did not dare go far out to sea. They were afraid of getting lost. They had no way of telling directions when it was cloudy. They could only tell directions when they could see the sun or the stars.

But about 500 years ago a great age of exploration began. Sailors dared go far out to sea. For they now had a way of guiding their ships. They had compasses. Their compasses were small magnets fastened so that they could turn around easily.

A compass made of a magnet—a magnetic compass—tells direction because the earth acts as a great magnet. The earth's magnetic force pulls a compass magnet, or needle, into a north-south position.

No one knows who made the first compass. Some think that the Chinese did. Others say that it was invented in Italy.

Some of the early compasses were little pieces of lodestone resting on small pieces of wood or cork which floated in a bowl of water. Lodestone is a kind of iron ore. Another name for it is magnetite. Pieces of lodestone are natural magnets. After men learned to make magnets of steel, they could make better compasses.

The picture below shows a pocket compass. The compasses used on ships are larger and more complicated. Modern magnetic ship compasses are usually made of several magnets fastened to a flat disk called a compass card. The card is mounted on a pivot so that it can swing around freely. The card and the pivot are in a glass-covered bowl usually filled with an alco-

A Pocket Compass

hol mixture on which the card floats. The liquid keeps the card from swinging as the ship sways from side to side. The magnets pull the card around and tell the directions.

Telling exact direction from a compass is not easy. For in most places a compass needle does not point exactly north. It points to the north *magnetic* pole, which is several hundred miles from the true North Pole. Charts help sailors correct their compass readings so that they can tell true north.

In many big boats of today another kind of compass is also used. It is a gyroscope compass, or gyrocompass. A compass much like it is used in airplanes. (See GYROSCOPE; MAGNETS; NORTH POLE.)

Compasses aided the exploration of the New World.

	1680	1690	1700	1710	1720	1730	1740	1750	1760	1770	1780	1790	1800	1810

JOHANN SEBASTIAN BACH   1685—1750   Christmas Oratorio;

FRANZ JOSEPH HAYDN   1732—1809

WOLFGANG AMADEUS MOZART   1756—1791

LUDWIG VAN BEETHOVEN   1770—1827

FRANZ SCHUBERT   1797

FELIX MENDELSSOHN

FREDERIC CHOPIN

ROBERT SCHUMANN

FRANZ LISZT

RICHARD WAGNER

GIUSEPPE VERDI

CÉSAR FRANCK

JOHANN STRAUSS

STEPHEN FOSTER

JOHANNES BRAHMS

GEORGES BIZET

PETR ILICH TSCHAIKOWSKY

ANTON DVOŘÁK

EDVARD GRIEG

NICOLAS RIMSKY-KORSAKOFF

ENGELBERT HUMPERDINCK

MAGIC FLUTE

TOY SYMPHONY

MARRIAGE OF FIGARO

COMPOSERS The story of our music of today begins with Johann Sebastian Bach. This great composer lived more than 200 years ago. Most of his music was written for the organ. Since Bach's time there have been many great composers. Some have written for one instrument, some for another. Some have written for whole orchestras. Some have written songs and operas instead of instrumental music.

The work of a composer is difficult. It requires great skill and much practice. Anyone who wants to become a composer must thoroughly understand the techniques of music and how to use them to express happiness, sadness, excitement, contentment, and many other human feelings. He must try to get the listener to feel these moods through his music. He must know perfectly all the sounds that can be created by the different instruments of an orchestra. He must weld these different sounds together to form a work of art.

The chart names a few of the great composers. It shows when they lived and gives the names of one or two of their works. Some of these men lived long lives. Others died young. Some were happy. Others lived lives full of sorrow and trouble. Some were famous while they lived. Fame did not come to others until long after they died. But they all wrote great music. (See BACH, JOHANN SEBASTIAN; MUSIC; OPERAS; OPERETTAS; ORCHESTRA.)

1820	1830	1840	1850	1860	1870	1880	1890	1900	1910	1920	1930	1940	1950	1960

Well Tempered Clavichord

Toy Symphony; Surprise Symphony

Marriage of Figaro; Don Giovanni

Fifth Symphony; Moonlight Sonata

1828   Unfinished Symphony; Serenade

1809—1847   Song without Words; Wedding March

1810—1849   Minute Waltz; Funeral March

1810—1856   The Two Grenadiers; Traümerei

1811—1886   Liebestraum; Hungarian Rhapsodies

1813—1883   Lohengrin; Tannhäuser

1813—1901   Aida; Rigoletto

1822—1890   Symphony in D Minor

1825—1899   The Blue Danube

1826—1864   Old Black Joe; My Old Kentucky Home

1833—1897   Cradle Song

1838—1875   Carmen

1840—1893   Nutcracker Suite

1841—1904   New World Symphony

1843—1907   Peer Gynt Suite

1844—1908   Scheherazade

1854—1921   Hansel and Gretel

GIACOMO PUCCINI   1858—1924   La Bohème

EDWARD MacDOWELL   1861—1908   Woodland Sketches

CLAUDE DEBUSSY   1862—1918   Afternoon of a Faun

JAN SIBELIUS   1865—1957   Finlandia

SERGEI RACHMANINOFF   1873—1943   Second Piano Concerto

GEORGE GERSHWIN   1898—1937   Rhapsody in Blue

DMITRI SHOSTAKOVICH   1906—   First Symphony

THE BLUE DANUBE

CRADLE SONG

RIGOLETTO

NUTCRACKER SUITE

COMPOUNDS Just a list of all the substances in the world would take many books the size of this one. And all of these substances are made up of only about 100 simple substances called elements. Most of the millions of substances are compounds or mixtures of compounds. A compound is made of two or more elements joined together.

The smallest bit of an element is an atom. The smallest bit of a compound is a molecule. Every molecule of a compound has atoms of at least two kinds in it.

No one can tell just by looking at a compound what is in it. Water is a compound everyone knows. It is made up of hydrogen and oxygen. They are both colorless gases! Sugar is even more surprising. It has oxygen and hydrogen in it just as water has. It has carbon in it, too. Carbon is usually black. Soot is carbon. Carbon is not sweet. Neither is hydrogen or oxygen. But sugar, of course, is.

A molecule of a compound is always made up of just so many atoms of each element in it. Carbon dioxide is one of the gases in the air. It is harmless. In fact, plants could not grow and make food for us if there weren't any carbon dioxide in the air. A molecule of carbon dioxide is made up of two atoms of oxygen and one atom of carbon. Carbon monoxide is made up of carbon and oxygen, too. But it has only one atom of oxygen for each atom of carbon. It is a very poisonous gas.

Scientists have a shorthand way of writing the names of compounds. H_2O is water. The figure "2" shows that there are two atoms of hydrogen to every atom of oxygen. $C_{12}H_{22}O_{11}$ is cane sugar. In a molecule of cane sugar there are 12 atoms of carbon, 22 atoms of hydrogen, and 11 atoms of oxygen. CO_2 is carbon dioxide. CO is carbon monoxide.

The picture shows four other compounds. They are salt, quartz, carbon tetrachloride, and red oxide of mercury.

Salt (NaCl) is made of sodium, a poisonous metal, and chlorine, a poisonous gas. Salt is not at all like either element. It is not poisonous. In fact, our bodies have to have it to stay alive.

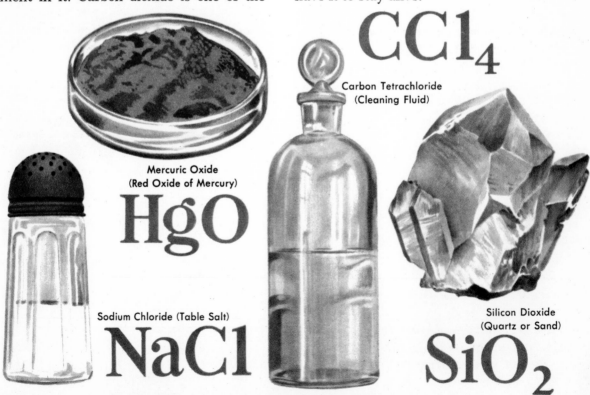

CCl_4
Carbon Tetrachloride
(Cleaning Fluid)

Mercuric Oxide
(Red Oxide of Mercury)
HgO

Sodium Chloride (Table Salt)
NaCl

Silicon Dioxide
(Quartz or Sand)
SiO_2

Tons of concrete were poured into forms to make this great dam.

Quartz (SiO_2) is a very common compound—one of the commonest in the world. It is made of oxygen and silicon. Not many people have ever seen pure silicon. But almost everyone has seen this compound of silicon. For most grains of sand are tiny bits of quartz.

HgO is red oxide of mercury. Who would guess that this red powder is made of the silvery liquid mercury and colorless oxygen? And who would guess that colorless carbon tetrachloride (CCl_4) is made of black carbon and the greenish gas chlorine?

New compounds are being made every day. Elements are being joined in new ways. Finding new ways of making elements join together has given us some wonderful new materials. Among them are the plastics. (See ATOMS; CHEMISTRY; ELEMENTS; MOLECULES.)

CONCRETE Many great dams are made of concrete. Thousands of miles of roads and sidewalks are made of concrete. There are concrete floors and foundations in many buildings. Concrete is one of our most important building materials.

Cement, water, sand, and crushed rock or gravel are mixed together to make ordinary concrete. Usually big machines do the mixing. The rock "batter" is then poured into wood or steel molds which give the concrete the shape wanted. When the concrete hardens, the mold can be taken away. A concrete wall or walk or dam can be made in much less time than it would take to build it of blocks of stone.

Concrete can also be made into blocks and then built into buildings. Many small houses are made of concrete blocks.

There are special kinds of concrete for special uses. Sometimes steel rods are run through it. Then it is called reinforced concrete. Concrete floors may have asphalt added so that they will be more comfortable to stand on. For lightweight concrete, rock materials lighter than sand and gravel are used. Pumice, a very light rock formed from lava, is one. Vermiculite is another. Vermiculite concrete may weigh only one-eighth as much as concrete made with sand and gravel.

Concrete is strong, and it lasts well. It will not burn. Termites and borers cannot eat it. And concrete is cheap, compared to many other materials. No wonder it is popular. (See ASPHALT; BUILDING MATERIALS; DAMS; ROADS AND STREETS.)

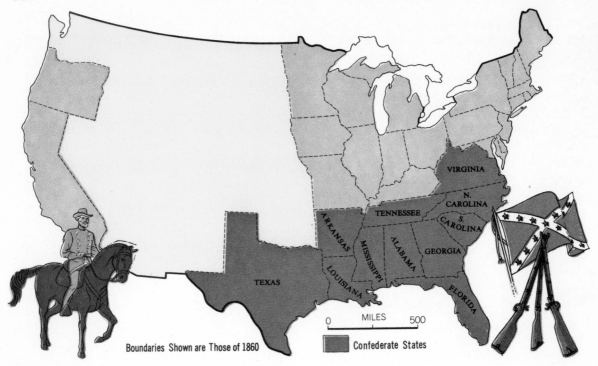

Boundaries Shown are Those of 1860   MILES   0   500   Confederate States

CONFEDERATE STATES In 1860 there were 33 states in the United States. But in December of that year South Carolina withdrew, or seceded, from the Union. In the first months of 1861, 10 more southern states seceded. They were Alabama, Arkansas, Florida, Georgia, Louisiana, Mississippi, North Carolina, Tennessee, Texas, and Virginia. These states formed the Confederate States of America. They chose Jefferson Davis as their president and Richmond, Va., as their permanent capital.

These southern states wanted to set up a government of their own because they did not agree with the northern states about a number of things. One of the big disagreements was about slavery. The South thought that it could not do without slaves. The North was against slavery.

A bitter war was fought between the North and the South. The Confederate States lost the war. They became once more a part of the United States of America. (See EMANCIPATION PROCLAMATION; LEE, ROBERT E.; LINCOLN, ABRAHAM; MASON AND DIXON'S LINE; MONITOR AND MERRIMAC; SLAVERY.)

CONFUCIUS (551-479 B.C.) Twenty-five hundred years ago life in China was very hard. Robbers roamed the countryside. The government was weak and not always fair. Most of the people were hopelessly poor. Into these times one of China's great leaders was born. His name in Chinese was K'ung-fu-tse. We call him by a Latin form of that name, Confucius.

Confucius came from a noble family, but his parents were poor. His father died when Confucius was only three years old. The boy was a good and obedient son to his mother. He grew up to be quiet, thoughtful, and studious.

As Confucius watched the people around him, he became eager to help them. At last he left his family and started out to teach others how to live better lives. He taught his pupils to be honest and kind, to honor their parents, and to obey their rulers. He taught them that a good man never lets himself get angry. He taught them that one should accept his fate meekly, no matter what that fate was.

Many of his sayings were gathered together and written down. They are somewhat like the proverbs in the Bible. One of his sayings is much like our Golden Rule. "Do not do unto others," it says, "what you do not wish others to do to you."

Because he was so wise, Confucius was made the chief justice of a province. He did his work very well. But another government official plotted against him. Confucius chose to go into exile rather than stay and fight. He did not believe in fighting. For years he wandered from province to province spreading his ideas to all who would listen to him.

Confucius never pretended to be more than an ordinary man. But after he died great temples were built to him. His beliefs make up one of the world's great religions—Confucianism. There are over 300,000,000 followers of Confucius today. (See RELIGIONS OF THE WORLD.)

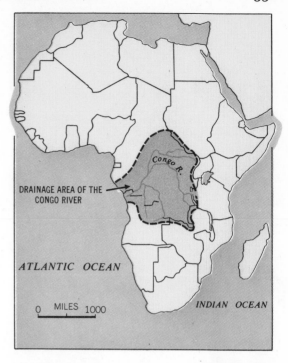

DRAINAGE AREA OF THE CONGO RIVER

ATLANTIC OCEAN

0   MILES   1000

INDIAN OCEAN

CONGO RIVER Africa has several great rivers. One is the Congo. The Congo River is one of the 10 longest rivers in the world. In places this big river is six miles wide. In other places it is narrow and flows through a deep gorge.

The Congo starts not far from where the Nile River begins, but it flows in a different direction. The Nile flows 4,000 miles to the north, the Congo 3,000 miles to the west. The Congo empties into the Atlantic. On its way it crosses the equator twice.

Most rivers as big as the Congo have built great deltas where they reach the sea.

The Congo has no delta. As it enters the sea it flows too swiftly to drop mud.

There are few cities on the banks of the Congo. Traveling down this vast river would not be at all like traveling down the Mississippi. These are some of the strange sights a traveler might see: hippopotamuses and crocodiles in the water; elephants in high grass near the banks; hot, gloomy forests with bright flowers, chattering monkeys, and screaming parrots; African natives catching fish with long spears; huts made of grass and palm leaves; the blazing sun hanging almost straight overhead at noon.

In the Congo there are many falls and rapids which boats cannot pass. Railroads for passengers and freight have been built around some of them. Big ocean ships can sail about 100 miles up the river—up to the first falls. Above these falls small boats are used.

Nearly 500 years ago a Portuguese explorer discovered the Congo. He gave it the name *Poderoso*, which means "the mighty." It is a good name for this great river. (See AFRICA; BELGIUM; DELTA; JUNGLES; PYGMIES; RIVERS; RUBBER.)

CONIFERS IN THE UNITED STATES

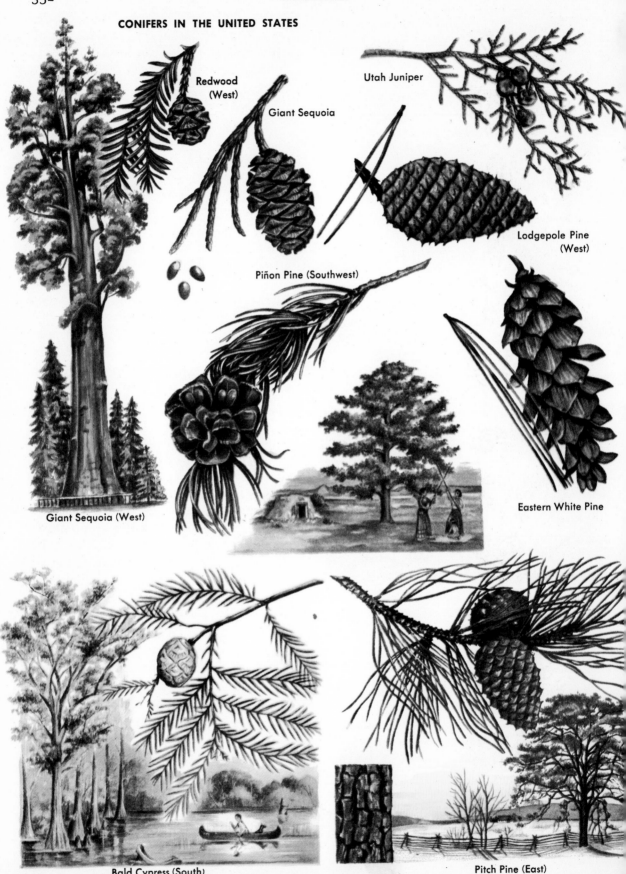

Redwood (West)

Giant Sequoia

Utah Juniper

Lodgepole Pine (West)

Piñon Pine (Southwest)

Eastern White Pine

Giant Sequoia (West)

Bald Cypress (South)

Pitch Pine (East)

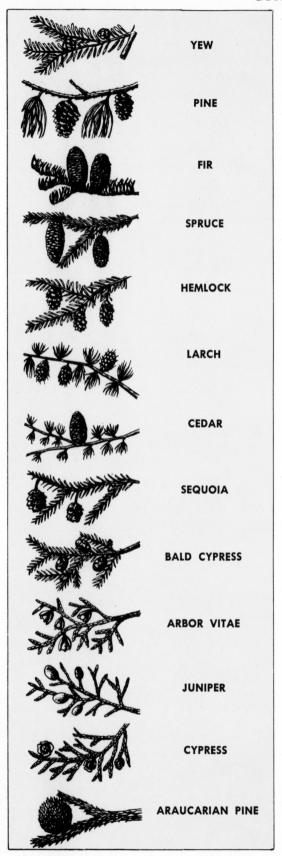

YEW

PINE

FIR

SPRUCE

HEMLOCK

LARCH

CEDAR

SEQUOIA

BALD CYPRESS

ARBOR VITAE

JUNIPER

CYPRESS

ARAUCARIAN PINE

CONIFERS At Christmas time conifers play a big part in our celebrations. For our Christmas trees are conifers.

"Conifer" means "cone-bearer." Most conifers produce their seeds in cones. A few have berrylike fruits instead.

Scattered over the world are hundreds of kinds of conifers. Not all of them are trees. Some junipers, for instance, are bushes which grow close to the ground. But most conifers are trees. Among them are the giants of the plant world—the redwoods and the big trees, or sequoias. Among them, too, are many of our most important timber trees.

The chart on this page shows the chief groups of conifers. Some of these groups are not found in the United States. The araucarian pines are South American trees. We call some American conifers "cedars," but the true cedars are found only in the Old World.

Most conifers are evergreens and do not drop their leaves when winter comes as elms and maples do. But some conifers do lose their leaves in the fall. The larches and the bald cypresses, for example, are conifers, but they are not evergreens.

Some conifer leaves are scalelike and lap over one another. Others are so narrow they are called needles. The needles of different conifers are not alike. Some are short; others are long. Some are four-sided; others are flat. Some grow in bunches of two or more; others are not bunched. There are differences in color, too.

The evergreen conifers do not keep the same leaves all their lives. They keep losing old leaves a few at a time instead of losing all of them at one time in the fall.

Great conifer forests once covered a large part of the United States. Millions of trees have been cut for lumber. Millions more have been killed by forest fires. One of America's problems now is how to keep her conifer forests from disappearing. (See BIG TREE; CONSERVATION; LUMBERING; WOOD.)

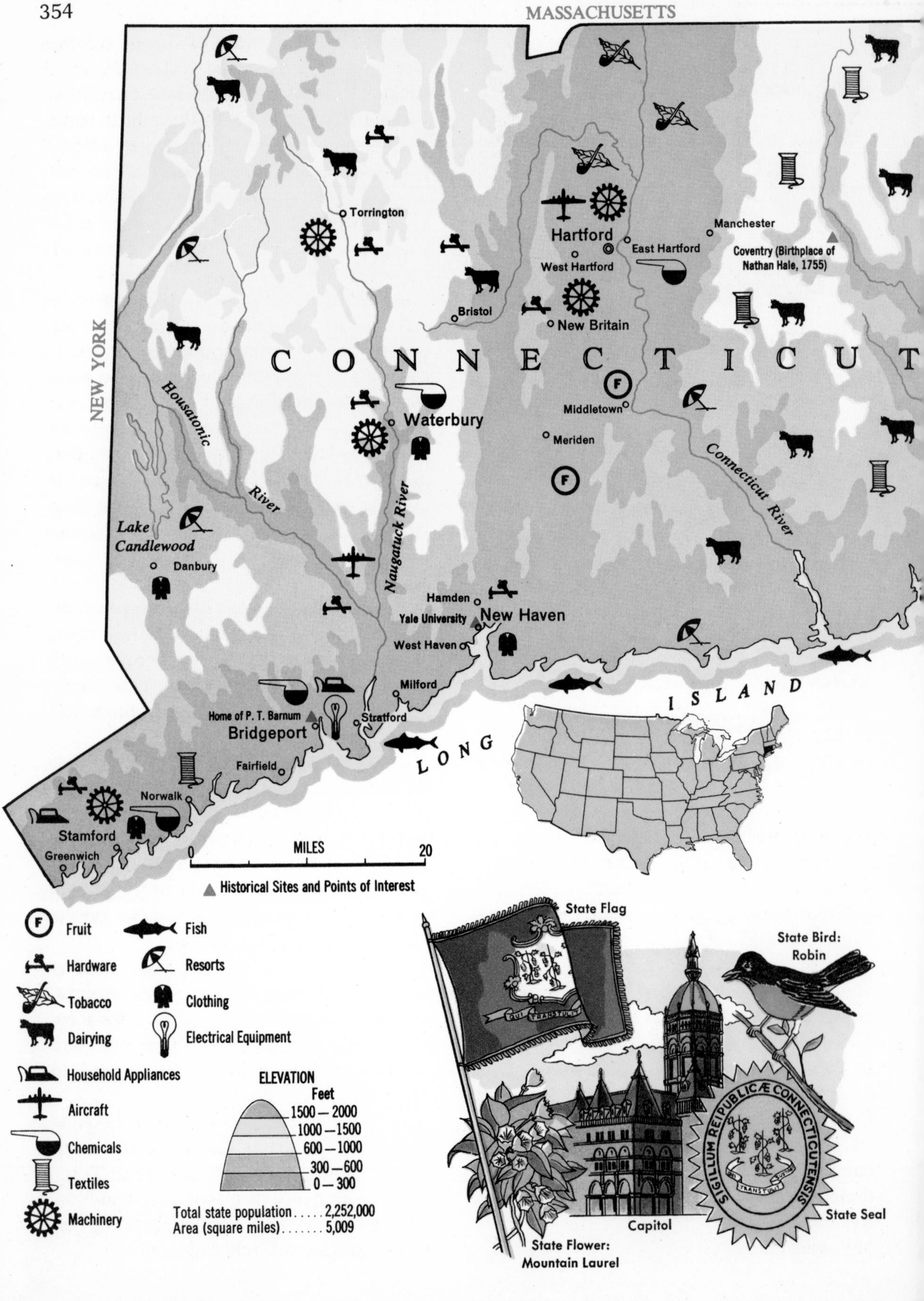

MASSACHUSETTS
NEW YORK
CONNECTICUT
Torrington
Hartford
West Hartford
East Hartford
Manchester
Coventry (Birthplace of Nathan Hale, 1755)
Bristol
New Britain
Middletown
Meriden
Waterbury
Housatonic River
Naugatuck River
Connecticut River
Lake Candlewood
Danbury
Hamden
Yale University
New Haven
West Haven
Milford
Home of P. T. Barnum
Bridgeport
Stratford
Fairfield
Norwalk
Stamford
Greenwich
LONG ISLAND
MILES
0
20
Historical Sites and Points of Interest
Fruit
Fish
Hardware
Resorts
Tobacco
Clothing
Dairying
Electrical Equipment
Household Appliances
Aircraft
Chemicals
Textiles
Machinery
ELEVATION
Feet
1500 — 2000
1000 — 1500
600 — 1000
300 — 600
0 — 300
Total state population..... 2,252,000
Area (square miles)....... 5,009
State Flag
QUI TRANSTULIT SUSTINET
State Bird: Robin
SIGILLUM REIPUBLICÆ CONNECTICUTENSIS
State Seal
Capitol
State Flower: Mountain Laurel

Atomic Submarine
New London

RHODE ISLAND

Covered
Bridge

Instrument
Making

Quinebaug River

Shetucket R.

Norwich

st American Ship built here in 1664
New London

Whaling
Museum
Mystic

Village
Church
Spire

O U N D

CONNECTICUT Ever since there has been a United States, Connecticut has been a famous little state in it. The seacoast of this state in southern New England borders Long Island Sound. And the huge city of New York is just beyond the southwestern corner of the state.

Connecticut's main rivers flow southward into the sound. At their mouths are good harbors. In many streams there are falls, for both the eastern and western parts of the state are very hilly. But the central part is lowland. And southward across it the very long Connecticut River flows. In Indian language, the word "Connecticut" means "upon the long river."

Only two of the 49 states are smaller than little Connecticut. But quite a few states—21—have fewer people. Connecticut has a great many cities, but none of them is really large. The surrounding countryside has many beautiful tree-covered hills and many lowland and valley farms.

Connecticut was one of the 13 colonies that united to form the United States. A nickname for the state is Constitution State. In 1639, people in three little settlements on the Connecticut River adopted the first constitution of its kind in America. Almost 150 years later, parts of the Constitution of the United States were made much like that constitution for the colony of Connecticut.

In colonial days, many little factories were located at falls in the rivers where water power was plentiful. Connecticut factories were the first in America to make men's hats, needles and pins, brass buttons, hooks and eyes, clocks and watches, coffee grinders, and cookbooks. Peddlers carrying these useful articles on wagons or in packs sold them throughout New England. Where little factories were built earlier, cities and big modern factories now stand. The state is famous for the manufacture of brass articles. Airplane construction ranks high. Even submarines using atomic power are built on Connecticut's coast. Things as different as carpets, silverware, firearms, and sewing machines now come from its factories.

Connecticut's capital and biggest city is Hartford. In that city there are the main offices of so many insurance companies that it is called a world insurance capital. Yale University in New Haven, Connecticut's second-biggest city, is very old and very great. Connecticut is famous for its schools and educational work.

About a fifth of Connecticut's land is used for farming. In the broad valleys, farmers produce dairy products, tobacco, poultry, and vegetables for themselves and people who live in cities. Much goes to New York City.

Today many people who work in New York have homes in southwestern Connecticut. The great new Connecticut Turnpike is a long link in a New England-New York highway system. Connecticut keeps on adding to its great achievements.

There are fewer swamps left for the cranes.

CONSERVATION Some of the early settlers in America came to the region near the James River in Virginia. They cleared away the trees there and planted big fields of tobacco. Tobacco takes a great deal from the soil. Soon the land was no longer able to produce big tobacco crops. Then the settlers moved on to new land. There was plenty of it. The story of these planters has been told in just a few words: "Cut down, wear out, walk off."

When settlers first reached the Great Plains they found huge herds of bison, or buffaloes. There were so many bison that a hunter might take home for food only the tongues—the choicest meat—of most of the bison that he killed.

These are samples of the way early settlers wasted the riches they found in America. The wasting went on for more than 200 years. At last people began to see that it must be stopped, or in time there would be no riches left. They began to do something about conservation. Conservation is using without waste.

Soil and wild life are two of the natural riches Americans wasted. Among the others are forests, water, and minerals such as coal and oil.

Americans have wasted soil in two ways. They have worn it out just as the early Virginia planters did. They have also let it be washed away. The Mississippi River alone carries several hundred million tons of soil a year and dumps it in the sea. Water running into streams after heavy rains makes gullies. Gullies can turn good farmland into land that cannot be farmed at all.

The bison is only one of the wild animals that have been killed in enormous numbers. Some kinds of animals—the passenger pigeon, for instance—have been entirely killed off.

This ghost town used to be a thriving lumber town.

People have not only killed many animals. They have taken homes away from many by cutting down forests and plowing up grasslands. They have dumped wastes into streams and made them unfit for fish. They have drained marshes where water birds used to live.

The early settlers had to cut down trees to clear land for farming. People have kept on cutting down trees so fast that virgin forests—forests from which no trees have been cut—are almost gone. Of course, trees that are made into houses, furniture and other useful things are not wasted. But Americans have destroyed many trees needlessly, partly by starting forest fires.

Water covers nearly three-fourths of the earth. It is hard to believe anyone has to think of saving it. But much of the earth's water is salty. In many places fresh water is scarce. By cutting down forests and plowing up grasslands, people have made it easy for rain and snow water to run off instead of sinking into the ground. There is always water standing underground. The top of this water is called the water table. In large parts of America the water table is getting lower.

Americans have mined their minerals wastefully, without stopping to think that it took millions of years for the minerals to collect in the earth. Once the storehouse is empty, it will take millions of years to fill it again.

What can be done? In many cases the harm already done cannot be undone. But much can be done to prevent waste in the future. And some of the damage done can be repaired. Worn-out farmland can be built up with fertilizers into good land again. Forests can be replanted. Streams can again be made fit for fish.

The United States Government has done a great deal to stop waste. Many laws have been passed. Forest preserves and national parks have been set up. Rangers guard against forest fires. Farmers are taught how to plow their land so that the soil is

Pink Salmon

Chum Salmon

Salmon are protected by fishing laws.

not as easily washed away. Game laws protect wild life. Fish hatcheries raise young fish to be put into the lakes and streams. Great dams have been built to store up water. The story of what the government is doing is a long one.

But laws do not help unless people obey them. Plans are of no use unless people follow them. Conservation is not something that can just be turned over to the government. Everyone has a part in it.

Of course, the United States is not the only country that is interested in conservation. No country can afford to waste the riches nature gave it. (See BISON; CROP ROTATION; EROSION; FISHING; FORESTS AND FORESTRY; NATIONAL PARKS AND MONUMENTS; PASSENGER PIGEON; SOIL; WATER SUPPLY.)

Some hunters would kill a buffalo just for its tongue.

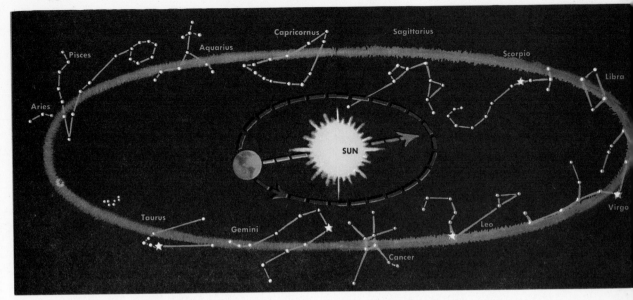

The zodiac, or circle of animals, as it seems to encircle the solar system

CONSTELLATIONS The stars we see as we look up at the sky at night are not scattered evenly across the whole sky. Instead, they are in groups. A group of stars is called a constellation. "Constellation" means "stars together."

The people of long ago saw the constellations as pictures in the sky. The names they gave the constellations tell us what pictures they saw. Most of the constellation names we use came down to us from the Greeks and Romans. Among them are Taurus (the Bull), Canis Major (the Big Dog), Pegasus (the Winged Horse), Draco (the Dragon), Ursa Major (the Big Bear), and Ursa Minor (the Little Bear).

There are constellations in every direction from the earth. But only from the equator can they all be seen. The star map on the next page shows many constellations. These are all visible in the United States. But in Argentina some of these constellations are never visible.

What constellations we see when we look up at the sky depends partly, then, on where we are on the earth.

The constellations on the map are all visible from the United States, but they can never all be seen at one time. The night sky changes with the seasons. It changes

because of the journey of the earth around the sun. No one sees Orion on the Fourth of July or Scorpio on Christmas Eve.

What constellations we see when we look up at the sky depends partly, then, on what time of year it is.

The night sky also changes from hour to hour. The turning of the earth makes some constellations seem to travel in a circle

It is expected that by 100,000 A.D., the stars of the present Big Dipper, moving in the direction of the arrows, will have formed the new shape below.

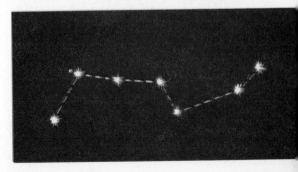

in the sky. Halfway between the equator and the North Pole, for instance, the Big Dipper is always visible, no matter what time of night it is. It seems to circle around the North Star. The farther north one goes, the more constellations there are that never disappear below the horizon. But in most places the turning of the earth makes some constellations rise in the east and set in the west. A constellation visible in the western sky just after sunset will have set by midnight, and other constellations will have risen in the east.

What constellations we see as we look up at the sky depends partly, then, on what time of night it is.

Stars are always moving. And the stars of a constellation are not always moving in the same direction. But the constellations are all so far away from us that no change in shape shows from one year to another. As thousands of years go by, however, they do change. The Big Dipper will look rather different in 100,000 years.

There are a great many star myths. They come from all parts of the world. The people of earlier times were not satisfied with simply naming the pictures the stars made. They made up stories to explain how each constellation came to be in the sky. (See ASTROLOGY; ASTRONOMY; PLANE-TARIUM; SKY; STARS; ZODIAC.)

The Constellations as They Would Appear Above the North Pole

Stars in Order of Brightness
1. Sirius
2. Vega
3. Capella
4. Arcturus
5. Rigel
6. Procyon
7. Altair
8. Betelgeuse
9. Aldebaran
10. Pollux
11. Spica
12. Antares
13. Fomalhaut
14. Deneb
15. Regulus
16. Castor

CONTINENT, LOST More than 2,000 years ago Plato, a famous Greek philosopher, wrote about a continent that he called "Atlantis." This continent, he said, had been west of the Pillars of Hercules, the gateway into the Mediterranean Sea. Its people had been highly civilized. But, a great earthquake had made this continent sink below the sea 9,000 years before Plato's time.

Probably Plato did not expect anyone to believe in Atlantis. But many people thought the story was true. Some people still believe in this lost continent. Whole books have been written about it.

Changes are, of course, always taking place in the earth's surface. Small islands have appeared and disappeared. Volcanic eruptions build up new mountains and tear the tops off old ones. Coast lines change.

Earthquakes are fairly common. But scientists have not been able to discover that any large amount of land has sunk below the sea in the past 100,000 years.

There are some signs that there was once a large island in the Atlantic where the small Azores are now. But this island, if there ever was one, disappeared 10 or 15 million years ago. That was long before there were any people living on the earth. Plato's lost continent, scientists are sure, was just a story.

There have been other stories like it. Less than 300 years ago, for instance, a sea captain brought to Scotland some people he said he had rescued from a wicked magician on an island west of Ireland. The island he called Hi-Brazil. The story was foolish, but for more than 100 years after that, Hi-Brazil was put on maps.

Eskimo

Polar Bear

Tropics

Antarctic Penguins

Reindeer

Northern Whale

Toucan

Toltec Ruins

Armadillo

W E S T E R N   H E M I S P H E R E

CONTINENTS A little less than one-third of the earth's surface is land. All the rest is covered with water. The land is not all joined together. There are thousands of islands. Besides, there are seven big "pieces" of land that are called continents.

The seven continents are North America, South America, Europe, Asia, Africa, Australia, and Antarctica. Australia and Antarctica are the only continents that are entirely separated by water from every other continent. North America and South America are joined to each other by a narrow neck of land. So are Africa and Asia. And Asia and Europe are joined together for such a long distance that they are sometimes called just one continent. The name given it is Eurasia.

Asia is by far the largest continent. In parts it is very crowded. More than half of all the people in the world live in the countries of Asia.

Australia is the smallest continent. And it is not crowded. But it does not rank lowest in population. Antarctica, which is larger than either Australia or Europe, has no people living in it at all. It is an ice-covered continent.

The chart below tells how the seven continents compare in size and population. The figures are in round numbers.

Continent	Size in Square Miles	Population
Africa	11,500,000	215,000,000
Antarctica	5,000,000	0
Asia	17,000,000	1,500,000,000
Australia	3,000,000	9,000,000
Europe	3,850,000	560,000,000
North America	8,500,000	235,000,000
South America	6,800,000	120,000,000

Siberian Bear

Walrus

Eiffel Tower

Chinese Pagoda

Rice Fields

African Lion

Australian Kangaroos

EASTERN HEMISPHERE

COOKING Imagine our meals if we did not cook any food. Celery and strawberries and many other fruits and vegetables are good uncooked. So is milk. But not many people would enjoy raw beefsteak or raw eggs or raw sweet corn. Besides, without cooking we could not have soups, bread, pie, cake, or cookies.

Cooking makes many foods taste better. It also makes many foods easier to digest. Cooking makes some foods much safer to eat, too, for the heat of cooking kills germs that may get in food.

No one knows when or how cooking began. Perhaps a very long time ago some fresh meat fell in a fire by accident. Soon it began to cook. It smelled very good. When the fire died down, the meat was taken out and tasted. It was so good that from then on many foods were cooked.

When white men first came to the New World the Indians were cooking in simple ways. This was one way: They built an open fire. When it had died down, they put pieces of meat wrapped first in leaves and then in mud in the hot coals. When the meat was done, they broke off the covering of baked mud and leaves.

This was another way the Indians cooked: They dug a pit in the ground and lined it with stones. They next built a fire in the pit and kept the fire going until the stones were very hot. They then raked out the ashes and put in the food. They covered it over, and the hot stones cooked it.

We still do some cooking for fun with open fires, but most of our cooking today is done with stoves of some sort. With our stoves we can cook food in many different ways. The chief ways are baking, roasting, frying, broiling, boiling, and steaming.

Baking means cooking in an oven. The meat we today call roasted is really baked. Originally, roast meat was cooked by hanging it over hot coals or in front of a flame.

When food is fried, it is cooked in fat on top of the stove. If it is cooked in deep fat, we say that it is French fried.

In broiling, slices of meat or other moist foods are cooked on a rack close to a flame or an electric burner. Dry foods like bread are toasted in the same way.

Most cooking in colonial times was done over an open fire. The cook of today has a gas or electric stove. Modern cooking is easier, cleaner, and quicker.

We boil food in water on the top of the stove. It is the heat of the boiling water and not the bubbling that cooks the food. Some foods are cooked over boiling water instead of in it. The steam that comes from the water does the cooking.

Much cooking with water is now done in pressure cookers. The tight-fitting lid of a pressure cooker holds in much of the steam from the boiling water. The water gets much hotter than boiling water usually is. Food cooks very fast in a pressure cooker because of the increased heat.

One secret of good cooking is to use the right amount of salt and other seasoning. Here are three other secrets:

Use the right amount of heat. Most stoves of today can be set to give the amount of heat that is wanted.

In boiling use as little water as possible.

Do not cook food too long.

COPERNICUS (1473-1543) The year before Columbus discovered America, Niklas Koppernigk entered the University of Cracow in Poland. He was to become almost as famous as Columbus, but not many people know him by his Polish name. He is known by his name in Latin—Copernicus.

Copernicus did not make himself famous by discovering a new continent. Instead he wrote a book about astronomy. It had so many new ideas in it that he is called the father of modern astronomy.

After Copernicus finished his work at the University of Cracow, he went to Italy to study. At Cracow he had become interested in astronomy. He wanted to learn more about it. In Italy he watched the stars and kept records of what he saw.

After a few years in Italy, Copernicus went back to Poland. He became a canon in the Cathedral of Frauenberg. But soon he was given permission to study in Italy again. He spent five years there studying astronomy and mathematics and medicine. In 1506 he returned to Frauenberg and spent the rest of his life there.

Copernicus had only crude instruments.

The duties of Copernicus as canon did not take all his time. He still had time to study astronomy. But Copernicus did not spend night after night in stargazing. He was more interested in trying to work out an explanation of what he had seen.

In his time people thought that the earth was the center of the universe and that the sun and all the stars turned around it. Very early in his study of astronomy Copernicus decided that this idea was wrong. He had these three ideas: The earth travels around the sun. The earth spins around as it travels. The earth is just one of the sun's family of planets.

Other learned people heard of these ideas. They wanted Copernicus to write a book about them. But Copernicus did not wish to do so. The Church, he knew, would not be pleased if he published a book saying that the earth was not the center of the universe. Many churchmen would call the idea a threat to religion.

But after many years Copernicus wrote the book. It was published in 1543. A copy of it reached him on the day he died. He did not live to see the great storm his book stirred up. His ideas seem so simple to us now that it is hard to understand why people fought so hard against them. (See ASTRONOMY; EARTH; SOLAR SYSTEM.)

COPPER AND ITS ORES

Native Copper

Chalcopyrite

Malachite

Copper Crystal

Azurite and Malachite Mixture

Azurite

After Cutting and Polishing

Open Pit Copper Mine in Southwestern United States

COPPER Of all the many metals, copper was one of the very first to be used by man. Only gold has been used as long. No wonder copper was discovered early. All that ancient man had to do was to pick it up from the ground. For copper, like gold, is often found in the earth as a free metal.

Not many metals are found free. Most of them are found only in ores. There they are mixed or joined with other materials. Getting metals out of their ores and refining them may be very hard. Copper is not by any means always found free. There are many copper ores.

At first ancient man probably prized copper just for its beauty. But soon he discovered that he could make much better tools of it than of stone.

While digging around in the earth for copper, ancient man must have found tinstone. In time he learned how to get the metal tin from it. By melting tin and copper together, he made bronze. Bronze is harder than copper and therefore more useful for tools and many other things. Still later, man found that by melting zinc and copper together, he could make brass. Mixtures such as bronze and brass are called alloys. Copper and bronze were man's most common metals until he learned how to get iron from its ores.

Most of the metal objects we use today are made of iron or steel. But copper is still widely used. Since, next to silver, it is the best conductor of electricity, copper is made into wire for carrying electric current. Almost every electrical appliance we use has copper in it. Copper carries heat well, too. Many cooking pans are part copper. Much copper is used in the building of ships because it does not corrode easily. In the ocean liner "Queen Mary" over 3,000,-000 pounds of copper and copper alloys were used.

Copper is used widely in art work. It has a beautiful color and can be given a high polish. The statues in our parks and public places are generally made of bronze. Many medals and coins are made of copper or its alloys. Buildings are sometimes trimmed with copper.

Today almost all the copper we use comes from copper ores. Most copper ores are blue or green. Copper is mined in many sections of the world. The picture shows one of the big copper mines in the United States. Carloads of ore are scooped up. They go to big smelters, where the copper is taken from the ore. (See ALLOYS; BRONZE; MINES AND MINING.)

COPYRIGHT Suppose a boy wants to print a small newspaper to sell to his friends. He reads the material about dinosaurs in this encyclopedia and decides to copy it in his paper. Is there any reason why he shouldn't? One word tells the answer. It is the word "copyright."

This word is on one of the first pages of every book printed in the United States. It means, "No one has a right to copy and sell this book or any part of it unless the author or publisher says that he may."

A copyright protects the author and the publisher of a book. Long ago, anyone could copy another author's work. In Shakespeare's time a printer might listen to one of Shakespeare's plays, write it down, and then print it and sell it.

To get a copyright in the United States the writer or publisher must send two copies of the work to the Copyright Office in Washington, D.C. He must also pay a small fee. The copyright he gets is good for 28 years. At the end of that time it may be renewed for another 28 years.

Any book can be copyrighted. So can magazines, paintings, drawings, maps, plays, sermons, speeches, pieces of music, photographs, and motion pictures.

CORAL For nearly half a billion years tiny animals called corals have lived in the earth's warm seas. We know about the corals of long ago because they left behind them millions upon millions of the rock "houses" they built for themselves.

Corals are simple animals, with no bones, no heads, and no legs. They wave food into their mouths with a circle of tiny feelers. Corals look much like little flowers. And as a rule they grow much as plants do. New animals branch off from old ones. Soon a whole colony is built up. Each animal takes in lime from the water and walls itself up with it. The older animals die, but their limestone houses remain.

There have been so many billions of billions of corals that in many places in the Pacific Ocean coral reefs rise in circles above the surface of the sea. These circles are called atolls. Many islands of the Pacific are bordered by coral reefs.

There are many different kinds of coral. The tiny animals themselves are all much alike. But the rock houses they build are quite different in shape. Brain coral, organ pipe coral, and staghorn coral are common kinds. Precious coral is red. Beads are often made of it. (See BERMUDAS.)

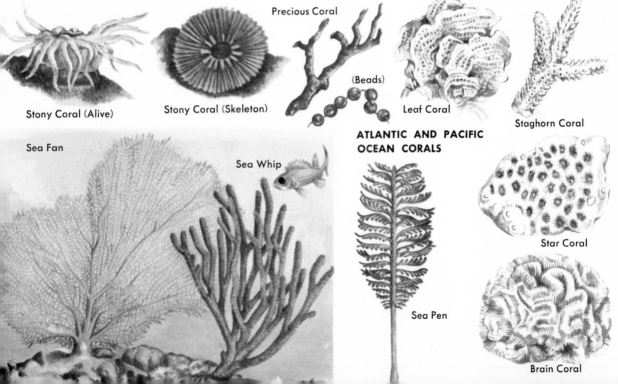

Stony Coral (Alive)

Stony Coral (Skeleton)

Precious Coral

(Beads)

Leaf Coral

Staghorn Coral

Sea Fan

Sea Whip

ATLANTIC AND PACIFIC OCEAN CORALS

Sea Pen

Star Coral

Brain Coral

Workmen cut cork from living trees

CORK Many medicine bottles have cork stoppers to keep the medicine from spilling. Life preservers are filled with cork. Cork is used for hot-dish plates. It is used in the caps of soft-drink bottles. Coasters to put under glasses of ice water are often made of it. So are some of the helmets which explorers wear in hot tropical lands. Artificial arms and legs are made of cork, too. Ground-up cork is used in linoleum. The centers of baseballs are cork. Cork is also placed between the double walls of refrigerators and cold storage rooms.

Cork is certainly very useful. Four things about it make it so. It is so light that it floats on water. It is waterproof. It is elastic. Heat cannot travel through it easily.

Cork comes from the bark of one kind of oak tree. The tree is the cork oak. Most trees have cork in their bark. But no other tree has so much as the cork oak.

A cork oak has to be 20 years old before its cork is worth cutting. If the cork is then cut off carefully, a new layer will grow. Every seven or eight years the cork can be cut again.

One big oak tree may furnish as much as 500 pounds of cork at a time. But most trees furnish much less.

The cork is boiled as a way of cleaning and softening it. The rough outer layer is then scraped off.

More than half of all the cork in the world comes from Portugal and Spain.

Ships sailing away from those countries very often carry cargoes of baled cork. Some cork is now raised in California, but the yields are not yet very large.

Buyers cut up the cork into the sizes and shapes they want. Some cork is cut so thin that 500 sheets would make a pile only an inch thick. (See BARK; TREES.)

CORN All except one of the grains raised in the United States came from the Old World. The one truly American grain is corn. Maize is another name for it. One region in the United States is called the Corn Belt because so much corn is raised there. Corn is an important crop in many other countries, too.

Corn is a grass just as wheat, rye, rice, oats, and barley are. But it grows to be much bigger than most of its relatives.

There is a big puzzle about corn. No one knows what wild plant it came from. There is no wild corn anywhere. There is not even a wild plant much like corn. Probably its ancestor lived in South America or Mexico, for the Indians there were raising corn long before Columbus discovered America. Its use spread northward. Friendly Indians brought corn to the Pilgrims and showed them how to plant it.

The kernels on an ear of corn are seeds wrapped in a thin covering. In each grain a baby plant lies in a bed of food, which is mostly starch. A corn plant has two kinds of flowers. The tassel at the top of the stalk is made up of flowers that furnish pollen. The flowers where the seeds form

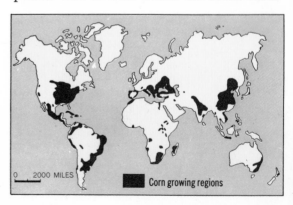
0   2000 MILES   ■ Corn growing regions

CORN PLANT

Leaf

Stalk

Roots

are lower on the stalk. The silks are parts of these flowers. Pollen must reach the silks before seeds can form.

Much corn is used as food for people. Much is used, too, as food for other animals. Besides, corn is used in manufacturing many things. Cornstarch, corn syrup, cooking oil, and wallboard are just a few of the things made from corn.

A great deal of the corn raised today is hybrid corn. Hybrid corn is a cross between different varieties. It usually produces much bigger crops than ordinary corn. (See CEREALS; FOODS; GRASSES; HYBRIDS; PLANT BREEDING.)

CORN BELT The Corn Belt is the part of the United States that leads in the growing of corn. The soil is rich, and the weather is good for corn. There are many summer showers. And the summer nights as well as the days are warm.

The Corn Belt might also be called the Hog Belt. For most of the farmers feed a great deal of the corn they raise to hogs. Many cattle are brought to the Corn Belt to be fattened, too. The old saying is true that "most of the corn goes to market on four feet."

The Corn Belt stretches from western Ohio to eastern Nebraska. Almost three quarters of all the corn grown in the United States comes from this area. Iowa is the leader, and this state is often called the "land where the tall corn grows." Corn is not the only crop grown on the farms in the Corn Belt, but always a great deal of the land is planted in corn. A traveler here sees so many cornfields that he does not need to be told that he is in the Corn Belt.

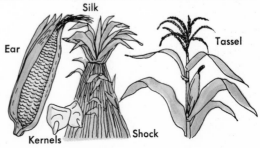

Silk

Ear

Tassel

Kernels

Shock

CORTÉS (1485-1547) Hernando Cortés was a boy in Spain at a thrilling time. Columbus made his first trip to the New World when Cortés was seven. Soon many Spaniards were on their way to the Americas to find their fortunes. Cortés made up his mind to go to the Americas, too. When he was 19, he sailed for the West Indies.

For several years Cortés stayed in the West Indies as a planter. Then for a time he was the mayor of a city in Cuba. But his real adventure began in 1518. In that year he set out with 11 ships and several hundred men to conquer Mexico.

The Aztec Indians, Cortés knew, had a rich kingdom in Mexico. The Aztec ruler was Montezuma II. He lived in a city built in the middle of a lake. It stood where Mexico City is now.

When Montezuma heard that the Spaniards were coming, he sent two nobles and 100 slaves to meet Cortés at the shore. The slaves brought many wonderful gifts. Montezuma wished to show that he was rich and powerful. Among the gifts there were plates of gold and silver as big as cartwheels, a helmet filled with gold dust, and armor decorated with solid gold.

Montezuma hoped the Spaniards would go home with these riches. But Cortés wanted more than ever to conquer this rich kingdom. To force his men to stay with him, he burned all his ships except one.

It was a long, hard trip from the place where he landed to the capital of the kingdom. There was much fighting along the way. Food was short, too. Montezuma kept sending messages urging the Spaniards to go back. But the messages did no good.

When Cortés neared the capital, Montezuma came to welcome him. The two pretended to be friends. Cortés was invited to the palace. As soon as he got there with his men, he made Montezuma a prisoner.

Montezuma tried to bribe Cortés with costly gifts.

The Aztecs rose up against Cortés and against Montezuma, too. They blamed Montezuma for letting himself be captured. In the fighting Montezuma was killed. Cortés escaped from the city. But soon he fought his way back and became the ruler of Mexico.

Other Spanish explorers became jealous of Cortés. In a few years the King of Spain sent out a new ruler to take his place. Cortés went back to Spain to plead his case. The King agreed that he could do more exploring, and could keep part of any riches he found. But he could not rule Mexico.

He did go back to Mexico, but he found no more riches. Instead, he lost what he had. Once more he returned to Spain for help. He got none. He died before he could return to the land he had conquered. (See AZTECS; MEXICO.)

Instruments sent aloft measure cosmic rays.

COSMIC RAYS About 50 years ago scientists noticed that odd things were happening to some of their experiments. Rays of a strange kind were reaching them. They were much like X rays, but they were not X rays. The scientists set out to track down the strange rays. They found that these rays came from far outside the earth. The rays were named cosmic rays.

Cosmic rays do not seem important to most of us. We do not see them or feel them. But scientists, of course, wanted to find out much more about them as soon as they found out there were such things. They went here, there, and everywhere to study them. They went into coal and iron and copper mines. They went into caves and into the great cracks in glaciers. They went deep down under the sea and up to the tops of high mountains. In balloons they went higher in the air than anyone had ever gone before. They even went into such out-of-the-way places as the mouth of a big cannon and under great piles of salt. Many turned diver or miner or mountain climber or airman. Some of these scientists even lost their lives exploring.

Cosmic rays are still mysterious. Scientists are not yet sure exactly where they come from. But what they have found out helps them to understand better the great universe around us.

Cotton Blossom

Cotton Boll

Cotton Seeds

COTTON A bouquet of cotton blossoms would be pretty. But no one picks cotton blossoms for bouquets. The blossoms are left on the cotton plants to form seeds. The seeds themselves are useful, but even more useful is the fluffy white cotton fastened to the seeds. About three-fourths of all the people in the world today wear cotton clothing.

Cotton must have a long growing season —200 days without frost. For that reason it grows only in warm climates.

The people of India raised cotton more than 3,000 years ago. The Indians of Peru and Mexico had fields of cotton in the days of the Spanish explorers. Now the United States raises more cotton than any other country in the world. All the southern states are cotton states. Arizona and California raise cotton, too. The cotton crop of the United States brings in more than two billion dollars a year.

Cotton seeds are planted in early spring. After the plants are fairly large, "cotton choppers" thin out the rows. Most cotton plants grow to be about three feet tall. Their flowers are white at first but soon turn red. Each flower forms a seed ball called a boll. The boll becomes about as big as an egg. When it is ripe, it opens. Then it looks like a snowball. In a cotton

This big sack will hold about 100 pounds of cotton.

field ripe bolls, green bolls, white flowers, and red flowers can all be seen at the same time.

Much cotton is picked by hand. But cotton-picking machines are being used more and more. After the cotton has been picked the seeds must be removed. Until Eli Whitney invented the cotton gin in 1793 the seeds were taken out by hand. The "iron fingers" of the gin do the work much faster.

The cotton is baled for sale. Cottonseed oil is squeezed from the seeds. It is used in such things as salad dressing and soap. The crushed seeds become cottonseed meal, a good food for cattle.

Cotton plants have many enemies. One of the most harmful is a beetle called the cotton boll weevil. The weevil lays its eggs inside the bolls. (See FIBERS; TEXTILES.)

COVERED WAGON Many pioneers crossed our great prairies and plains to the West before there were any railroads. Most of them traveled by covered wagon. Sometimes as many as a hundred covered wagons made the journey together so that there would be greater safety from Indian attacks.

The wagons were sturdy and had broad-rimmed wheels to keep them from sinking down in the mud. They were higher at both ends than they were in the middle. Each wagon had a great canvas cover that made it look top-heavy. The canvas covering was held up by arches of iron or wood. It could be drawn shut at the ends. If the people wished, a peephole could be left.

The covered wagons had to be big. They had to carry food for several weeks. Besides, they had to carry clothing and blankets, pots and pans, and other things, too. A family lived in its covered wagon very much as families live now in trailers.

Travel by covered wagon was slow, for the wagons were pulled, as a rule, by oxen. If there were several wagons together, there were usually some men on horseback. But they had to slow down to stay with the oxen.

As the wagons moved slowly through the waving grass of the prairies, they looked a little like boats bobbing on the sea. They were often called "prairie schooners." They had another name, too. It was "Conestoga (kon es TOE ga) wagon." This name came from the name of a town in Pennsylvania. Conestoga wagons were first made there. (See PIONEER LIFE IN AMERICA; PLAIN; PRAIRIE.)

Crater Lake is in the crater of an old volcano.

CRATER LAKE Not many lakes are at the tops of mountains. Crater Lake is. It is high in the Cascade Mountains in the crater of a dead volcano.

Crater Lake is one of the most beautiful lakes in the world. It is a lovely blue. High, steep walls made of lava surround it. In places the lava is twisted into odd and interesting shapes. Evergreen trees cover some of the walls.

The lake is about six miles long and four miles wide. Near one end a strange rocky island rises above the water. In the moonlight it looks like a ship under full sail. But when the moonlight strikes it in a certain way, the "ship" suddenly disappears. No wonder it is called Phantom Island. Another island is called Wizard Island. It is a little volcano with a crater at the top.

There are three puzzles about Crater Lake. For one thing it is about 2,000 feet deep—deeper than any other lake in the United States. For another thing, it is much larger than anyone would expect a lake in a crater to be. The craters of most volcanoes are much smaller than the big bowl that holds this lake. Besides, the water is fresh. This would not be surprising except that no streams have been found that run out of the lake. The water of other lakes with no outlet is salty. But not the water of Crater Lake!

Scientists have studied the lake, and this is the story they tell. It is the story of a vol-cano that swallowed its top. The volcano was once much higher than it is now. It had erupted time after time, and each eruption had built it higher. At last it was nearly two miles high. In between the eruptions there had been long times of quiet. They had been so long that rivers of ice had formed high up on the sides of the tall mountain and had moved slowly down its valleys.

At last the bottom of the crater sank, and the whole top of the mountain fell in. Probably what happened was that a great amount of hot, liquid rock down deep under the volcano was suddenly drained away. The floor of the crater sank almost halfway to the foot of the mountain. Of course, the crater was partly filled up by the material of the top of the mountain. But still the crater was very deep.

Water from rain and snow formed a lake in the crater. But the volcano was not yet completely quiet. There was another eruption, and Wizard Island was built.

This story of how a volcano swallowed its top explains why the crater is so big and so deep. It does not explain why the water of Crater Lake is fresh. Scientists think that there may be an underground channel that carries water away. (See NATIONAL PARKS; VOLCANOES.)

CRETE The island of Crete is in the Mediterranean Sea south of Greece. It is not a very big island compared with some others in the Mediterranean. Crete is 160 miles long, but only 7½ to 35 miles wide. It has a high ridge of mountains that go up to 8,000 feet. One of its mountains is Mt. Psiloritis, called Mt. Ida in ancient times. It played an important part in stories of Zeus, the king of the Greek gods.

We hear a great deal about ancient Egypt and ancient Babylonia. We do not hear nearly as much about ancient Crete. But back in the days when Egypt and Babylonia were leading centers of civilizations, the people of Crete were also highly civilized.

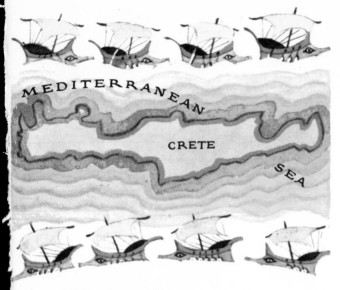

While the neighboring Greeks were still living in crude villages, the people of Crete had built beautiful cities with huge palaces. Four thousand years ago Crete was a busy, wealthy island.

There are ruins on the island now of many of the ancient towns and cities. In one city there are ruins of a vast royal palace. It is called the palace of Knossos (NOSS us). The king's throne in this palace is the most ancient one in all Europe. The palace covered what would amount to about four city blocks. Over the centuries earthquakes and fires have destroyed it. When the palace was built, there were hundreds of rooms in it. One of the rooms was the queen's bathroom. In it the queen's bathtub was found. In a nearby room there was a baby's bathtub. Pipes of clay tile carried water all over the palace. The kings and queens of Europe did not have such luxury for many, many centuries.

One of the myths of ancient Greece told that the son of King Minos of Crete was killed by the people of a town in Greece. As a punishment seven beautiful Greek maidens and seven Greek youths had to be sent to the king of Crete each year. They were fed to a monster called the Minotaur.

The Cretans were very talented in the arts, especially in architecture, fresco painting, and pottery.

Maynard Williams-Shostal
Minoan Fresco

Minoan Oil Jars   *Maynard Williams-Shostal*

Ruins of Palace of Minos   *Walter Guiber-Shostal*

Windmills Used for Irrigation

WINE

Mountaineer on a Mule

Octopus Fishing

Cheese

Grapes   Doughnut-shaped Bread   Olives and Olive Oil

This monster was kept in a labyrinth, a network of passages out of which it was very hard to find one's way. The Greek hero Theseus at last killed the Minotaur.

This story is just a myth. But there probably was a King Minos. The civilization of the ancient people of Crete is sometimes called the Minoan civilization. Its golden age was about 3,500 years ago.

Centuries before the Phoenicians became the great sea traders of the Mediterranean, sailors from Crete traveled far and wide over this big sea. The Cretans had learned from the Egyptians how to build boats. In their boats they carried wares for trade. Pottery made in Crete has been found in lands all around the Mediterranean. Probably the traders took ivory, among other things, in exchange for it.

The Cretans used their boats not only in trade but also in war. Their rulers are often called the "sea kings of Crete." Some of the seamen were really pirates.

The Cretans had tools and pots and pans made of bronze. They had jars of pottery so thin that they were like our eggshell china. Their artists carved beautiful figures in ivory. They made beautiful ornaments of gold, too.

Pictures on the walls in the ruins of Cretan cities tell us something about how the Cretans lived. They show boys and girls taking a bull by the horns and leap-

ing over its back. They show wrestling and dancing. They show ladies in fine clothes, shepherds guarding their flocks, and farmers gathering grain and grapes.

The Cretans could write, just as the Egyptians and Babylonians could. They wrote on clay tablets. But they used forms of writing which were all their own. For many years no one could figure out what the tablets said. But recently some of the writing has been read. The tablets that have been read, however, are just lists of people and commodities. When other Cretan writings have been translated, we may know much more about this ancient people.

The civilization of Crete began to decline more than 3,000 years ago. The island was conquered first by the Greeks and then by the Romans. About 1,100 years ago Moslems forced out of Spain invaded Crete. The island then became a hiding place for pirates who were feared all over the Mediterranean. The Greeks took over Crete again in A.D. 961. In 1669, after a siege of 20 years, the island fell to the Turks. Many of the Cretans became Mohammedans.

Today Crete is a part of Greece. It is a land of orchards and fields and pastures. The ancient ruins on the island were not uncovered until the early part of this century. Until then no one had guessed that Crete was an important stepping stone between the first civilizations and the civilizations of Europe. (See GREECE; HISTORY; MEDITERRANEAN SEA.)

Many believe Croesus made the world's first coins.

CROESUS (KREE sus)
"As rich as Croesus" is a common saying. Croesus was a real person, and he was very rich indeed. He was the King of Lydia about 2,500 years ago. Lydia was a country in Asia Minor.

Croesus was made rich by gold and silver that were washed from the sands of a river in his country. The first coins in the world are said to have been made from this silver and gold.

Croesus was a powerful king. When he heard that the King of Persia was getting ready to make war, Croesus was not greatly worried. But he sent messengers to a Greek oracle to ask how a war with Persia would turn out. The word brought back was that a great empire would be destroyed.

Croesus understood the message to mean that he would destroy the great empire of Persia. Instead, the empire that was destroyed was his own. While Croesus was taking his time getting ready to fight, the Persians swept in and conquered Lydia. Croesus became a captive of the Persian king. (See HISTORY; MONEY; PERSIA.)

CROP ROTATION
All crops use up minerals from the soil. A farmer cannot expect his soil to stay rich if he raises crops on it year after year and never puts any minerals back into it.

But how can a farmer put back into the soil the minerals his crops take out? He can use fertilizers. He can also follow a good plan of crop rotation. Crop rotation means changing crops in regular order.

Some crops take more of one material from the soil. Some take more of another. Any crop rotation is probably better than raising such a "heavy-feeding" crop as corn year after year. But to be good a crop rotation must add something to the soil.

Grass is often used in a crop rotation. Plowing it under adds what we call humus to the soil. Humus helps change minerals that plants cannot use into minerals that they can use.

Clover is an even better crop for building up soil. Clover has tiny bumps on its roots. In the bumps there are bacteria of a special kind. They take nitrogen from the air and change it to a mineral that the clover plant needs. If, after the clover seed has been harvested, clover plants are plowed under, this mineral is added to the soil. So is humus.

Clover is one of the plants called legumes (LEG umes). Alfalfa, sweet clover, and soybeans are legumes too. All legumes can be used to help keep soil fertile.

Crop rotation does more than keep soil from wearing out. It also helps in fighting weeds and insects. If wheat were raised in a field several years in a row, weeds that can grow easily in wheat fields and insects that eat wheat would get a better and better foothold. But if crops are changed often, such weeds and insects do not have as good a chance to get established.

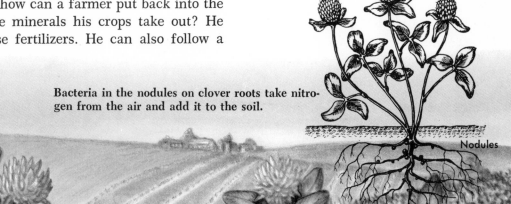

Bacteria in the nodules on clover roots take nitrogen from the air and add it to the soil.

Nodules

The Pope asked for recapture of the Holy Land.

CRUSADES When Jesus was alive, the Holy Land was a part of the great Roman Empire. A few centuries later it was in the hands of Moslems. For a long time these Moslems were friendly to Christians who came to visit the land where Christ had lived. But in 1071 the Turks captured Jerusalem. The Turks were Moslems, too, but they were not friendly to the Christians. Pilgrims on the way to the Holy City were sometimes beaten and robbed.

In 1095 the Pope called a great meeting. He asked his hearers to rescue the Holy Land. At once people flocked to do as he wished. "God wills it," men would shout as they dropped their work to start on their journey. In this way the wars called the Crusades began.

The name "Crusades" comes from the Latin word *crux.* It means "cross." Men on their way to fight for the Holy Land wore red crosses on their breasts.

The first groups that gathered would not wait till careful plans were made. One of these groups was led by a knight called Walter the Penniless. Another was led by Peter the Hermit. Some of the men in these groups were sincere Christians. Others were just vagabonds. Still others were trying to keep from being put in prison. These groups had no money. They had to beg their way. They were so eager to kill the Turks that they began killing Jews and others who were not Christians. In return many of them were killed. Few lived to reach the Holy Land.

The first really planned crusade was led by noblemen who were trained warriors Among them were Godfrey of Bouillon (boo YON), Robert of Normandy, and Robert of Flanders. Their army reached the Holy Land and, after much fighting, captured Jerusalem. But they did little to show that they were Christians. They massacred both Moslems and Jews. Before many years the Turks gathered an army and retook part of the land they had lost.

In the next two centuries there were several other Crusades. Between the second and the third Crusades the Turks under Saladin recaptured Jerusalem itself. The third Crusade was led by two kings—Richard the Lionhearted of England and Philip of France—and an emperor—Frederick Barbarossa of Germany. Frederick Barbarossa was drowned. Philip returned to France. Richard conquered part of the Holy Land but failed to win Jerusalem.

Another attempt to rescue Jerusalem was the Children's Crusade. Thousands of children joined to try to do what warriors had not been able to do. But none of them reached the Holy Land. Many died of disease or of hunger. Some were sold as slaves. Some turned back before it was too late.

There are many exciting stories of the Crusades. Pictures of Crusaders with their chargers and armor and banners are thrilling. But the whole story of the Crusades is not, it is clear, a very pleasant one. In the end the Holy Land was in the hands of the Turks just as it had been at the start.

But, although the Holy Land was much the same after the Crusades as before, Europe was not. The Crusaders brought back from the East spices and satins and riches of other kinds. More important, they brought back new ideas. Their gloomy castles no longer seemed wonderful. They wanted a better way of living and they set about getting it. The Crusades were failures as wars of conquest. But they pushed civilization in Europe ahead. They helped lift Europe up from the Dark Ages. (See HOLY LAND; JERUSALEM; KNIGHTHOOD; MIDDLE AGES; MOHAMMED.)

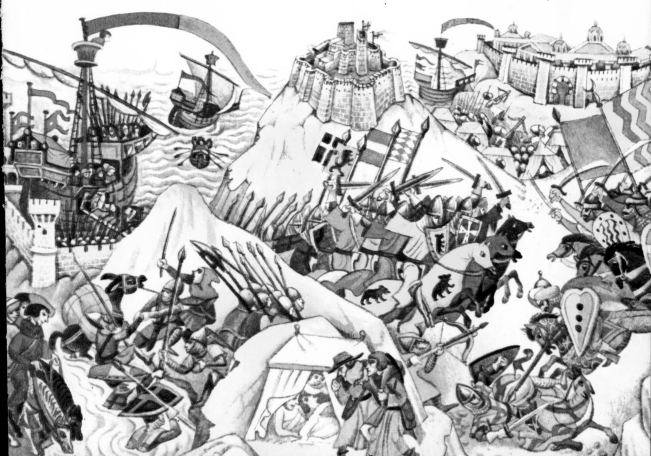

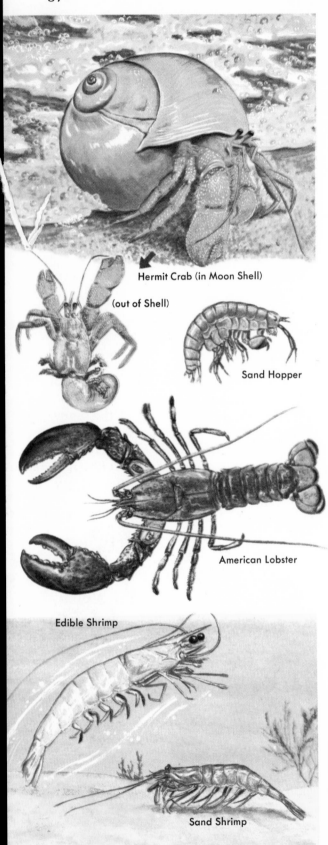

Hermit Crab (in Moon Shell)

(out of Shell)

Sand Hopper

American Lobster

Edible Shrimp

Sand Shrimp

CRUSTACEANS (krus TA shuns) Far more than half of all the kinds of animals in the world belong in the group of "jointed-legged" animals. This great group has in it the insects, the spiders, the centipedes, the thousand-legs, and the crustaceans.

There are not nearly as many crustaceans as there are insects, but there are thousands of kinds. The picture shows a few of the many kinds.

All crustaceans, like their insect relatives, have a protective covering of a remarkably tough material called chitin (KY tin). Crustaceans have two pairs of feelers. They breathe with gills.

Lobsters and crabs are fairly large animals. But some crustaceans are almost too small to be seen without a microscope. The water flea is one.

Most crustaceans live in salt water. But there are some in fresh water. The common crayfish is found in many ponds. And even though they are gill-breathers there are

Crayfish

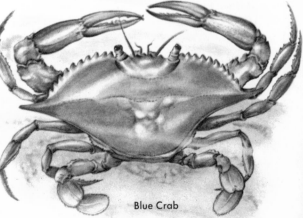

Blue Crab

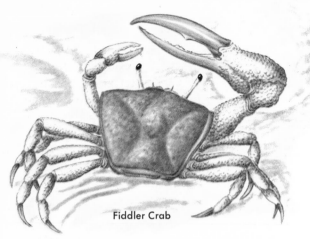

Fiddler Crab

crustaceans that live on land. The sow bug and the beach flea are land dwellers.

It is easy to see that the crayfish, shrimp, and lobster are close relatives. They are built on very much the same plan. They all have ten legs. Crabs have ten legs, too. The front legs of all these ten-legged crustaceans end in claws.

Most crustaceans move about freely. But barnacles fasten themselves to something solid when they are young and stay there the rest of their lives.

People eat lobsters, crabs, and shrimp. Even the crustaceans that we do not eat make good food for other animals. The very tiny ones are an important part of the "sea soup" many bigger animals live on.

Crustaceans have been on the earth for a very long time. Half a billion years ago the trilobites were the earth's leading animals. They were crustaceans. (See BARNACLES; LOBSTERS; TRILOBITE.)

CRYSTALS The pictures show several kinds of crystals. These crystals look as if someone had cut them into their shapes. But no one did. The minerals these crystals are made of form into these shapes without anyone's help. Every material that forms crystals has its own crystal shape.

Crystals are common. Every snowflake that falls in the wintertime is made of tiny crystals of ice. The grains of salt in our saltcellars are crystals. Rock candy is nothing but big crystals of sugar. The sugar in

our sugar bowls is made of smaller crystals. Grains of sand are crystals of quartz, but they have been battered about so much by wind and waves that their corners and edges have been worn off.

Some kinds of crystals are easy to make. Alum crystals, for instance, can be made in this way: First dissolve powdered alum in boiling water. Put in as much as the water will dissolve. Hang a string down into the solution. Then put the solution aside to cool. Cool water cannot hold as much alum as hot water can hold. Some of the alum will form crystals on the string. They will be like double pyramids.

But most kinds of crystals are not easy for people to make. Many crystals are formed in rocks when hot rock that rises from deep in the earth cools.

Some of the crystals found in rocks are so beautiful that we use them as gems. Usually, however, we do not use them in their own shapes. We cut them to make them the shape we want. Of all the many, many kinds of crystals, diamonds are the hardest. They are also, many people think, the most beautiful. (See DIAMONDS; GEMS; MINERALS; QUARTZ; ROCKS; SALT; SAND.)

Black Tourmaline

Beryl

Garnet

Rhodonite

Dogtooth Spar

Cuban Flag

Morro Castle

Tobacco

SUGAR

Coffee

Bananas   Pineapples

CUBA This island neighbor of the United States is sometimes called the "Sugar Island." The name is a good one, for sugar is Cuba's leading crop. Out of every ten acres that are farmed on the island, nearly seven are used for growing sugar cane. A person can drive for miles there through a "sea" of sugar cane. Some sugar plantations are big enough to have 100 miles of railroad on them.

Cuba has a good market for her sugar very close at hand. For the United States has the biggest sweet tooth of any country in the world. The people of the United States eat about 100 pounds of sugar per person each year.

Cuba is the biggest island of the West Indies, and it has many good harbors. It is about the size of Pennsylvania.

The climate of the island is excellent for sugar cane. Cuba is warm the year round. There is never any frost in its cropland. And rainfall is plentiful. Once in a while a hurricane strikes and does great damage. But Cuba is hit by hurricanes less often than some of its neighbor islands in the West Indies.

The soil of Cuba is especially good for sugar cane. It is also good for tobacco, bananas, pineapples, and coffee. Some cattle ranching is done, and copper, iron, nickel, and other minerals are mined.

About a million people live in Havana, the capital of Cuba. It has one of the finest harbors in the world. Long ago a large fort called Morro Castle was built to guard the entrance to the harbor. The old fort still stands, and is visited today by tourists.

Each year thousands of tourists visit Havana. The city has many historic buildings, and beautiful avenues, hotels, shops, and homes. Royal palms fringe its beaches. Many Cubans speak both Spanish—their own language—and English. Jai alai (HI a LI) and baseball are popular sports there.

Many of Havana's factories are cigar factories. Havana cigars are famous. Among the lovely things in its shops are leather articles made of alligator skin.

Cuba has had a troubled history. Columbus discovered the island on his very first voyage. He called it "the most beautiful land human eyes have ever seen." Soon one Spanish explorer after another reached its shores. The island became a part of the Spanish Empire.

The Spanish rulers of Cuba did not rule the island wisely. There was often trouble between them and the Cubans. Late in the 19th century Spanish rule became unbearable. The people of Cuba revolted. The United States helped the island win its freedom from Spain.

Even since Cuba won its freedom it has not always had good rule. But much has been done for the people. There are now free schools for all children. Both men and women can vote. Workers are better paid and do not have to work nearly as many hours as they used to work. Railroads and good roads have been built to bring all parts of the island closer together.

In one way it has not been good for Cuba to have its soil and climate so well fitted for raising sugar. So much land has been given to raising sugar that the prosperity of the island has depended too much on the price of sugar. Sugar prices change greatly. When they are high, Cuba is rich. When they are low, Cuba is poor.

Even when sugar prices are highest, the working people of Cuba are not as well off

GULF OF MEXICO

Andros I.

ATLANTIC OCEAN

BAHAMA ISLANDS

HAVANA

Matanzas

Santa Clara

Isle of Pines

Cienfuegos

Sancti-Spíritus

Camagüey

CUBA

CARIBBEAN SEA

Holguín

Bayamo

Manzanillo

Guantánamo

Santiago de Cuba

Windward Passage

JAMAICA

HAITI

Cocoa Beans

Sugar

Shipping

Tobacco

Dairying

Coffee

Fruit

Manganese

Iron

Chromite

ELEVATION
Feet
2000 — 5000
1000 — 2000
0 — 1000

Total population........5,829,029
Area (square miles).....44,217

MILES
0   200

Cuban Capitol

Jai Alai Player

Modern Hotel

Resorts

Crocodile

Cutting Sugar Cane

Oxcart

as one would expect. For much money from the United States and other countries has been put into the sugar plantations. Much of the profit, therefore, goes to people who do not live on the island.

In recent years steps have been taken to change Cuba from a one-crop land. Now not only tobacco but also coffee, cacao, and corn are coming to be important crops. Dairy farming and livestock raising are becoming important, too. There is a great deal of fertile land which is not yet cultivated. In the future, it is hoped, there will be fewer poor people in rich Cuba. (See COLUMBUS; CORTÉS; WEST INDIES.)

CURIE, MARIE (1867-1934), and **PIERRE** (1859-1906) The name Curie is famous. Pierre Curie and his wife, Marie, discovered radium. Radium is one of the earth's rare elements.

Marie Curie was born in Warsaw, Poland. Marie's three sisters and a brother were all older than she. The family was happy even though they were poor. But when Marie was eight, her oldest sister died. Two years later her mother died. Marie, however, was able to stay in school. When she finished high school she was given a gold medal for her good work.

Now Marie set to work to help her sister, Bronja, go to college. She gave lessons to the children of wealthy families.

By the time Marie was 24, Bronja had become a doctor and was married. Marie went to Paris to live with her and to attend the Sorbonne, a famous university.

After a few weeks Marie decided that she would have more time to study if she

Madame Curie in Her Laboratory

lived by herself. She moved to an attic room near the university. Often now she had only dry bread and tea to eat. A bunch of radishes or a bit of chocolate was a real treat. She studied very hard.

Then one day Marie met Pierre Curie, a French scientist and teacher. They fell in love and were soon married. Two years later their daughter Irene was born.

Marie had become interested in some strange rays certain rocks gave off. After much experimenting she decided that they must come from an element no one knew about. She made up her mind to find it.

Pierre was eager to help her. They agreed that if they found the new element they would call it radium.

They found it, but only after four years of very hard and discouraging work. Their laboratory was a leaky shack. It was almost unbearably hot in summer and miserably cold in winter. The Curies had decided to try to get radium from a rock called pitchblende. They had to handle tons of it.

Marie and Pierre knew that they had at last got a tiny bit of radium when they went back to their laboratory one night. The radium was glowing in the dark!

The Curies were given many honors. All the world praised them.

Soon after they made their famous discovery, a second daughter, Eve, was born. She was only two when Pierre was struck by a horse-drawn wagon and killed. Marie took her husband's place as a teacher.

Even though she had discovered radium and had showed others how to get it, Marie could buy very little of it for her own use in carrying on experiments. It was very, very expensive. She made two visits to America. Each time, to honor her, the American people gave her a gram of radium worth more than $100,000. Marie continued her experiments for many years. When she was 67, she died from the effects of too much exposure to radium, the very element she and her husband discovered. (See CANCER; ELEMENTS; RADIUM.)

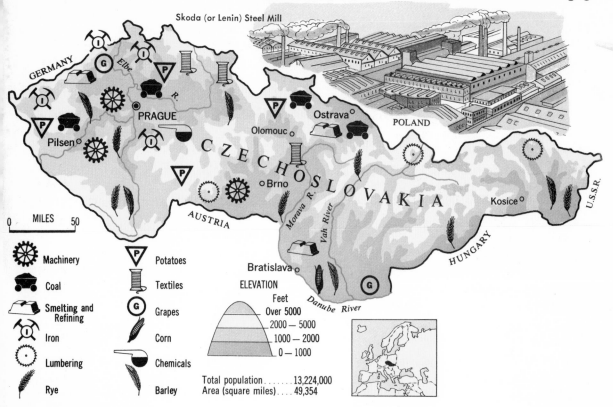

Skoda (or Lenin) Steel Mill

GERMANY
Elbe R.
PRAGUE
Pilsen
Olomouc
Ostrava
POLAND
C Z E C H O S L O V A K I A
Brno
Morava R.
Vah River
Kosice
U.S.S.R.
AUSTRIA
HUNGARY
Bratislava
Danube River

MILES 50

⚙ Machinery	P Potatoes	
Coal	🧵 Textiles	ELEVATION
Smelting and Refining	G Grapes	Feet Over 5000
I Iron	Corn	2000 — 5000
Lumbering	Chemicals	1000 — 2000
Rye	Barley	0 — 1000

Total population.......13,224,000
Area (square miles)....49,354

CZECHOSLOVAKIA When peace was made at the end of World War I, several new countries were formed in Europe. One was Czechoslovakia. A small part of this new country was carved out of Germany, a country defeated in the war. But most of it had been in Austria-Hungary, another of the defeated countries.

For centuries, Czech people and Slovak people had lived in the part carved from Austria-Hungary. The Czechs and Slovaks are closely related. Their languages are much alike. All through the time they had lived in Austria-Hungary, they had kept on using their own languages. And they had hoped very much to have a country of their own. Since the new country was the home of the Czechs and the Slovaks, it was named Czechoslovakia.

The people of the new Czechoslovakia began at once to work hard to make their country one they could be more and more proud of. They worked successfully for almost 20 years. Then, just before World War II, Germany was strong again and got

control of part of the country. And during that great world war, Czechoslovakia suffered much hardship.

At the end of that war, Czechoslovakia got back the land Germany had taken from it. But soon the influence of the Soviet Union was so powerful that a communist government was set up in Czechoslovakia. In 1948, the country became one of the communist-controlled countries back of the "iron curtain."

Czechoslovakia is almost exactly the size of the state of New York. It has almost as

Prague Athletic Arena

Castle on the Elbe

Tým Church
Prague

Carding Flax

Macocha Grotto
Moravia

Gathering Hay

Spejbl and Hurvínek
Puppet Theater
Prague

The Powder Tower
Prague

many millions of people, too. But from east to west it is longer than New York. And mountains form most of the country's western and northern boundaries.

The country is "land-locked." It has no seacoast at all. But two great rivers form highways to the sea. One is the Elbe. It flows from the western part of the country to the North Sea. The other is the Danube. It flows southeast to the Black Sea, and is the southern boundary of central Czechoslovakia. Bratislava, the second-biggest Czechoslovak city, is a Danube port. Important railroads cross the country. One that runs northeast to the Baltic Sea goes through the mountain pass called the Moravian Gate. Travelers have used that "gate" for centuries.

Most of the Slovaks live in Slovakia, the eastern part of the country. In it, cities and factories are fewer than they are farther west. The Slovaks are mostly farmers, shepherds, or lumbermen.

Most of the Czechs live in the richer western part of Czechoslovakia called Bohemia. It has fine forests, good farm lands, great stores of iron not far from coal, clay suitable for making china, and sand suitable for glassmaking. It has gold, silver, uranium, and other minerals, too. Mills widely known as the Skoda steel works are among the largest in Europe. Bohemian glass and Bohemian porcelain are famous all over the world. So is Bohemian beer. One of the most important crops raised on Bohemian farms is sugar beets.

Long, long ago, Bohemia was a kingdom. Its capital was Prague. Today Prague is Czechoslovakia's capital, its biggest city, and an Elbe port. The palace that was once the home of the kings of Bohemia is still standing. The Týn Church is one of Prague's famous ancient buildings. Its university was founded centuries ago. Parts of Prague are bustling and modern. Parts are quaint and quiet. It is one of Europe's most interesting cities. (See DANUBE RIVER; WORLD WAR I.)

B